Justice and Injustice in Law and Legal Theory

The Amherst Series in Law, Jurisprudence, and Social Thought

Each work included in The Amherst Series in Law, Jurisprudence, and Social Thought explores a theme crucial to an understanding of law as it confronts the changing social and intellectual currents of the late twentieth century.

Justice and Injustice in Law and Legal Theory

Edited by
Austin Sarat and Thomas R. Kearns

Ann Arbor
THE UNIVERSITY OF MICHIGAN PRESS

First paperback edition 1998
Copyright © by the University of Michigan 1996
All rights reserved
Published in the United States of America by
The University of Michigan Press
Printed and bound by CPI Group (UK) Ltd, Croydon, CR0 4YY

2001   2000   1999   1998   4   3   2   1

A CIP catalog record for this book is available from the British Library.

Library of Congress Cataloging-in-Publication Data

Justice and injustice in law and legal theory / edited by Austin
    Sarat and Thomas R. Kearns.
        p.   cm. — (Amherst series in law, jurisprudence, and social
    thought)
    Includes index.
    ISBN 978-0-472-09625-1 (sqb)
    ISBN 978-0-472-06625-4 (pbk)
    1. Law—United States. 2. Law—Philosophy. 3. Justice.
I. Sarat, Austin.   II. Kearns, Thomas R.   III. Series.
KF210.J87 1996
340'.1—dc20   96-9973
                                                         CIP

    ISBN 978-0-472-02368-4 (electronic)

Acknowledgments

We are grateful to our colleagues Lawrence Douglas and Martha Umphrey, with whom we share a commitment to the continued development of law as a subject of study in the liberal arts. *Justice and Injustice in Law and Legal Theory* is the subject of a course taught by Thomas Kearns. We thank the students in that course for their invigorating interest in many of the issues taken up in this volume. Finally, we would like to express special appreciation to the Keck and Arthur Vining Davis Foundations for their generous financial support.

Contents

Legal Justice and Injustice: Toward a Situated Perspective

Thomas R. Kearns and Austin Sarat

Did someone say justice was possible?
　　—Thomas Kennan, "Deconstruction and the Impossibility
　　　　　　　　　　　　　　　　　　　　　　　of Justice"

Running throughout the history of jurisprudence and legal theory is a recurring concern about the connections between law and justice and about the ways law is implicated in injustice. Commentators from Plato[1] to Derrida[2] have called law to account in the name of justice, asked that law provide a language of justice, and demanded that it promote, insofar as possible, the attainment of a just society. They have done so, however, in relentlessly abstract and general language, as if the demands of justice could only be apprehended accurately outside of history and context, and as if only philosophers were fit to engage in conversation about justice. The justice that is spoken about is, as a result, elusive, if not illusory, and disconnected from the embodied practices of law.

The essays collected in *Justice and Injustice in Law and Legal Theory* seek to remedy this situation by embedding inquiry about justice in an examination of law's daily practices, its institutional arrangements, and its engagement with particular issues at particular moments in time.[3]

---

1. See, for example, Plato's *Republic,* trans. G. M. A. Grube, rev. C. D. C. Reeve (Indianapolis: Hackett Publishing Co., 1992), Books I and IV, especially.

2. Jacques Derrida, "Force of Law: 'The Mystical Foundation of Authority,'" *Cardozo Law Review* 11 (1990): 919.

3. We have explored some of these themes in an earlier volume in this series. See Austin Sarat and Thomas R. Kearns, *Law in Everyday Life* (Ann Arbor: University of Michigan Press, 1993).

They move discussion from abstract philosophical argument toward concrete historical examples and, in so doing, broaden the conversation to include anthropologists, historians, and those engaged in struggles over specific legal questions. They do so by carefully examining the practices of law in order to identify moments when justice is realized.

Yet these essays also recognize that all too often law, in this culture and elsewhere, is a tool of injustice.[4] For every step taken toward realizing the good, an equal, if not greater, number of steps have been taken in the name of evil. As a result, in the study of law "injustice," as Judith Shklar argues, "should not be treated intellectually as a hasty preliminary to the analysis of justice."[5] According to Shklar, "[T]he real realm of injustice is not in an amoral and prelegal state of nature. It does not appear only on those rare occasions when a political order wholly collapses. It does not stand outside the gate of even the best known states. Most injustices occur continuously within the framework of an established polity with an operative system of law, in normal times."[6]

The essays in this volume present case studies in which the question of legal justice is contextualized. They use that question to examine particular issues and institutional practices and, in so doing, they make the question of justice come alive as a concrete political question. They refuse to get bogged down in philosophical abstraction or empty definitional exercises; instead, they recognize that, like liberty and equality, justice is yet another notion at the very center of Western political, social, and legal thought whose boundaries are notoriously indistinct, ill-defined and incessantly contested.[7] In so doing, they call on all of us to enter a dialogue about the justice and injustice of law.

In an earlier day, speaking about law and justice was not so vexing or difficult. Justice (*jus* meaning "law") was a legal term, pure and simple.[8] At the outset, then, "justice was defined and constituted by laws

4. For two examples, see Robert Cover, *Justice Accused: Antislavery and the Judicial Process* (New Haven: Yale University Press, 1975) and Peter Irons, *Justice at War: The Story of the Japanese American Internment Cases* (New York: Oxford University Press, 1983).

5. Judith Shklar, *The Faces of Injustice* (New Haven: Yale University Press, 1990), 19. Also Edmond Cahn, *The Sense of Injustice: An Anthropocentric View of Law* (New York: New York University Press, 1949) and Robert Folger, ed., *The Sense of Injustice: Social Psychological Perspectives* (New York: Plenum, 1984).

6. Shklar, *Faces of Injustice,* 19.

7. W. B. Gallie, *Philosophy and the Historical Understanding* (New York: Schocken Books, 1964), 527.

8. See Frank H. Knight, "On the Meaning of Justice," in *Justice,* ed. Carl J. Friedrich and John W. Chapman (Englewood Cliffs, N.J.: Prentice-Hall, Inc., 1963), 1.

which were 'given' and held to be unchanging and unchangeable."[9]
This ineluctable link between justice and law had the virtue of making
the boundaries of justice more or less clear; but it had the considerable
vice of labeling even heinous, iniquitous laws just. Justice could do no
critical or reconstructive work because it was impossible to think of justice as external to law.

Hobbes to the contrary notwithstanding,[10] most natural law
thinkers have resisted this result by insisting that unjust laws are not
law,[11] though doing so meant the end of any easy identification of positive or human law with "real" or binding law. The alternative, em-
braced by perhaps a majority of those who continue to be at ease in this
idiom, is to cut justice and law free from one another, to insist that justice is more than mere conformity to law[12] and to acknowledge that
even unjust laws might nonetheless be law.[13] Most recently, the distance
between law and justice has been recognized in postmodern theorizing
about ethics.[14] Thus, as Douzinas and Warrington argue,

> [J]ustice has the characteristic of a promissory statement. A
> promise states now something to be performed in the future. Being
> just always lies in the future, it is a promise made to the future, a
> pledge to look into the event and the uniqueness of each situa-
> tion. . . . This promise, like all promises, does not have a present

---

9. For the proposition that law defines justice, see Thomas Hobbes, *Leviathan* (Indianapolis: Bobbs-Merrill Co., Inc., 1958).

10. Ibid., 119–20.

11. Thomas Aquinas, *Summa Theologica*, ed. William Baumgarth and Richard Kegan
(Indianapolis: Hackett, 1988). For a more recent formulation of this position, see Robert P.
George, *Natural Law Theory: Contemporary Essays* (Oxford: Clarendon Press, 1993). See also
John Finnis, *Natural Law and Natural Rights,* (Oxford: Clarendon Press, 1890), and Russell
Hittinger, *A Critique of the New Natural Law Theory* (Notre Dame: University of Notre Dame
Press, 1987).

12. Plainly, the Greeks did precisely that by arguing that justice should be understood first and foremost as a property of persons, not of institutions or laws; it is clear, too,
that the link between law and justice also is ruptured by those many who would insist
that the concept of justice applies directly to the affairs of the family without, necessarily,
any reference to law.

13. See H. L. A. Hart, *The Concept of Law* (Oxford: Clarendon Press, 1961), chap. 9.
Compare with Lon Fuller, *The Morality of Law,* rev. ed. (New Haven: Yale University Press,
1964), chaps. 2 and 3.

14. See, for example, Drucilla Cornell, "Post-Structuralism, the Ethical Relation, and
the Law," *Cardozo Law Review* 9 (1988): 1587. Also her book *The Philosophy of the Limit* (New
York: Routledge, 1992).

time, a time when you can say: 'there it is, justice is this or that.' Suspended between the law and the good . . . , justice is always still to come or always already performed.[15]

Severance of the definitional tie between justice and law has left both notions free (if also bound) to acquire new identities.[16] In both cases, former boundaries were enlarged. Thus, matters other than those directly regulated by law (for example, the distribution of wealth) were viewed as falling under the purview of justice, and patently unjust legal arrangements (for example, apartheid in South Africa) were accepted as lawful despite their moral repugnance.[17] But this definitional separation by no means has put an end to the commonplace conviction that the principal home of justice is law and the special concern of law, perhaps its principal business, is justice. As Clarence Morris notes, "Though there can be law without justice, justice is realized only through good law."[18] In fact, law and legal theory continue to be shaped by concerns about justice and injustice, just as understandings of these notions are shaped by an awareness of law and the concerns of legal theory.[19]

By what might fairly be regarded as an accident of intellectual history, the deep connections between justice and law have been somewhat muted in that form of contemporary discourse which seeks to expand

---

15. Costas Douzinas and Ronnie Warrington, "The Face of Justice: A Jurisprudence of Alterity," *Social and Legal Studies: An International Journal* 3 (1994): 23. As Thomas Keenan asks, "Doesn't the appeal to a universal justice of the future, with which to counter the evident violence of today and tonight threaten precisely this erasure of the alterity of the future (which is to say its futurity) which the thought and promise first opens?" See "Deconstruction and the Impossibility of Justice," *Cardozo Law Review* 11 (1990): 1680.

16. Jack Balkin, "Being Just With Deconstruction," *Social and Legal Studies: An International Journal* 3 (1994): 393.

17. On the moral repugnance of apartheid, see Geoffrey Bindman, *South Africa: Human Rights and the Rule of Law* (London: Pinter Publishers, 1988).

18. Clarence Morris, "Law, Justice, and the Public's Aspirations," in *Justice*, ed. Carl Friedrich and John Chapman (New York: Prentice-Hall, Atherton Press, 1963), 170. In another essay in the same volume, Iredell Jenkens suggests that "justice is the form of order that man seeks to create through law." See Jenkens, "Justice as Ideal and Ideology," at 217.

19. See, for example, Ronald Dworkin's seminal essay on law and the model of rules in *Taking Rights Seriously* (Cambridge: Harvard University Press, 1977), particularly the second chapter, titled "The Model of Rules I." Here it is plain that Dworkin seeks an account of law that will meet certain minimal elements of justice. Conversely, J. R. Lucas is intent on explaining how laws can be unjust though nonetheless valid and obligatory; see his *On Justice* (Oxford: Clarendon Press, 1980). Theories of law and theories of justice often, though not always, work in tandem or in constructive tension.

the sphere of justice talk beyond the legal. They have been swamped by a preoccupation with distributive justice, a subject whose contemporary preeminence can unquestionably be attributed to John Rawls's *A Theory of Justice*.[20] "Justice," Rawls contends, "is the first virtue of social institutions, as truth is of systems of thought."[21] But the justice he has in mind is almost exclusively distributive justice, not justice more broadly construed; and distributive justice, he perhaps rightly implies, is not *peculiarly* the concern of law at all.

Similarly, Agnes Heller introduces the notion of a broad, though incomplete, "ethico-political concept of justice."[22] In her view, justice is not simply about principles of distribution; it concerns the perspectives, principles and procedures for evaluating institutional norms and rules. Developing themes in Habermas's communicative ethics, Heller suggests that justice is a key attribute of citizenship in which persons deliberating about problems confront them collectively in their actions without domination and with mutual tolerance of difference.[23] Iris Young expands on even this notion of justice, concluding that "the concept of justice coincides with the concept of the political,"[24] and while it is "not identical with the concrete realization of these values in individual lives,"[25] justice is attentive principally to "the degree to which a society contains and supports institutional conditions necessary for the realization" of the values of equal worth as these are promoted or confined in a society's basic institutional arrangements.[26]

Despite these broad and encompassing views of justice, the fact remains that justice is generally thought to be involved in the more limited matters of procedure, punishment, and recompense.[27] Thus, while law in its legislative moments might share with other social institutions

---

20. John Rawls, *A Theory of Justice* (Cambridge: Harvard University Press, 1971). It is, of course, reckless to attribute the focus in question entirely to an intellectual event; surely the maldistribution of the world's resources is a coordinate contributor to this effect.

21. Ibid., 3.

22. Agnes Heller, *Beyond Justice* (New York: Basic Books, 1987), 54.

23. *Ibid.*, 260–70. See also Iris M. Young, *Justice and the Politics of Difference* (Princeton: Princeton University Press, 1990), 33; and Jurgen Habermas, *The Theory of Communicative Competence*. Vol. 2, *Life World and System* (Boston: Beacon Press, 1987), 240–41.

24. Young, *Justice and Difference*, 34. Also at 9.

25. Ibid., 37.

26. Ibid.

27. Aristotle, *Nicomachean Ethics*, trans. Terence Irwin (Indianapolis: Hackett Publishing Co., 1985), chap. 5; and Lucas, *On Justice*, chaps. 4 and 5.

certain distributional objectives, it is generally thought that law has a separate and distinctive tie to justice, located most conspicuously, though not exclusively, in matters of form and process. By focusing attention on the distributional concerns of social institutions generally, Rawls's remarkable book sheds little light[28] on the special relationships that obtain between the concerns of justice and the more particular concerns of law.[29]

If not to Rawls, where might one turn to learn about justice in law? Perhaps there is no better place to begin than with the universal icon of justice (which is invariably associated with law), namely, the statue of Justicia, the blindfolded bearer of sword and balance. Despite certain ambiguities,[30] Justicia presumably embodies law's central link to justice, *impartiality*. The instrument of Justicia is a balance, not a scale, so it is only a comparative rather than an absolute measurement that is involved,[31] and she is blindfolded to prevent her decision from being inappropriately influenced or determined by forces of fear, bias, or favoritism. Moreover, she is blindfolded—not blind—suggesting a self-

---

28. There are some, of course, who hold that it sheds little light on the requirements of distributive justice *generally*, for, as Alasdair MacIntyre argues, the so-called "demands" of justice are always relative to some particular conception of rationality and agency. See *Whose Justice? Which Rationality?* (Notre Dame: University of Notre Dame Press, 1988), chap. 1.

29. The further important point returned to later in this chapter is that too narrow a focus on distributional concerns emphasizes persons as "possessors and consumers" rather than "doers and actors." As noted by Young, *Justice and Difference*, viewing persons from the latter perspective focuses attention on the fact that they seek many values, not just fairness in the distribution of goods—among them, learning and using satisfying skills, participating in forming and running social institutions, playing and communicating with others, and expressing one's feelings and perspective on social life in a context where others can and are apt to listen. In Young's view, "social justice concerns the degree to which a society contains and supports the institutional conditions necessary for the realization of these values" (37).

Young is joined in her qualms about the inadequacy of distributional accounts of justice by Michael Walzer, *Spheres of Justice* (New York; Basic Books, 1983) and *Interpretation and Social Criticism* (Cambridge: Harvard University Press, 1987); Michael Sandel, *Liberalism and the Limits of Justice* (Cambridge: Cambridge University Press, 1982); Heller, *Beyond Justice;* and Bruce Ackerman, *Social Justice and The Liberal State,* (New Haven: Yale University Press, 1980).

30. See Dennis E. Curtis and Judith Resnik, "Images of Justice," *Yale Law Journal* 96 (1987): 1727.

31. One must also note the presence of the sword for what it tells us about the nature of law and legal justice. Robert Cover, "Violence and the Word," *Yale Law Journal* 95 (1986): 1601; and Austin Sarat and Thomas R. Kearns, "A Journey through Forgetting: Toward a Jurisprudence of Violence," in *The Fate of Law,* ed. Austin Sarat and Thomas R. Kearns (Ann Arbor: University of Michigan Press, 1991).

willed refusal of vision. Justice, it seems, is a denial of sight though not of seeing, a regulation of information though not of knowing, a restriction on what is permissibly attended to though not a deficit of attention. As Derrida puts it, "Justice as the experience of absolute alterity is unrepresentable, but it is the chance of the event and the condition of history. No doubt an unrecognizable history . . . for those who believe that they know what they are talking about when they use this word. . . ."[32]

Justicia's blindness and balance takes the form of an aporia in which legal judgment is both free and yet bound to follow rules and prescriptions. "A just and responsible decision," Douzinas and Warrington contend, "must both conserve and destroy, or suspend, the law enough to reinvent it and rejustify it in each case. Each case requires a unique interpretation which no rule can guarantee absolutely. But, at the same time, there is no just decision if the judge does not refer to law or rule. . . . This is the reason that we cannot say that a judgment is just. A decision . . . cannot be declared just because justice is the dislocation of the said of law by the-unrepresentable-saying of ethics."[33] It seems reasonable to suggest that the blindfolded Justicia refuses representation, her refusal being itself a statement of the impossibility of bringing the Good into sight and translating it into legal judgment. As Derrida says, "From this point of view, justice would be the experience that we are not able to experience."[34]

Alternatively, following Curtis and Resnik, "[p]rocedure is the blindfold of Justice."[35] The proposition that procedure is itself an aspect of justice takes us some distance toward the further result that law and justice are ineluctably linked. Thus, to the extent that one supposes that the rule of law and the principle of legality are constituted largely by a commitment to regularized, self-limiting procedures, it is but a short step to the conclusion that procedural justice is inextricably tied to law itself.[36]

Along some such path, it seems possible to argue further that pro-

---

32. Derrida, "Force of Law," 971.

33. Douzinas and Warrington, "Face of Justice," 23. See also Derrida, "Force of Law," 961: "To be just, the decision of a judge . . . must not only follow a rule of law or general law, but must also assume it, approve it, confirm its value, by a reinstituting act of interpretation, as if ultimately nothing previously existed of the law in every case. . . ."

34. Derrida, "Force of Law," 947.

35. See Fuller, *Morality of Law*; Joseph Raz, *The Authority of Law* (Oxford: Clarendon Press, 1979), chap. 11; and J. R. Lucas, *On Justice*, chaps. 4 and 5.

36. See Fuller, *Morality of Law*.

cedures themselves must meet additional normative requirements, sounding in fairness and desert, and other dimensions of justice. As Hart has observed, a rule that is regularly, uniformly applied to prohibit certain minorities from using the town park might, despite its unfailing enforcement, be viciously unjust.[37] Legal justice, then, involves more than general observance of the rules that regulate exercises of legal authority; the rules themselves must be fair, eschewing wholly arbitrary distinctions between and among the persons to whom they apply or on whom they finally have effect; the rules must provide suitable forms of what, in the United States, are known as requirements of due process and equal protection.

Beyond form and process, then, the substance of law and legal judgments are themselves properly judged as just or unjust, where justice is an as yet unrealized aspiration for the good. "Laws," Balkin argues,

> apportion responsibility, create rights and duties, and provide rules for conduct and social ordering. Law is always, to some extent and to some degree, unjust. At the same time, our notion of justice can only be articulated and enforced through human laws and conventions. We may have a notion of justice that always escapes law and convention, but the only tools we have to express and enforce our idea are human laws and human conventions. Our conception of the just relies for its articulation and enforcement on the imperfect laws, conventions and cultural norms from which it must always be distinguished.[38]

Having envisaged ways of connecting law and justice, definitionally and aspirationally, it must be granted that not everyone regards the imagined association as an unalloyed good. Hayek, among others,[39] is persuaded that social justice is a mirage, a misguided affection, the pursuit of which threatens not only liberty but, eventually, law itself.[40] A

---

37. Hart, *Concept of Law*, chap. 8.

38. Balkin, "Being Just with Deconstruction," 16.

39. F. A. Hayek, *Law, Legislation and Liberty*. Vol. 2, *The Mirage of Social Justice* (London: Routledge, 1982).

40. In broad outline, the argument is this: we lack the knowledge to regulate complex economic arrangements efficiently by means of stable, discoverable rules. The effort to replace the guidance of spontaneous market adjustments by regulation will inevitably require ad hoc interventions and adjustments, which in turn will entail a diminution of

somewhat more moderate concern is that the demands of distributive justice and the rule of law are inevitably at odds with one another so that the successes of the one necessarily entail the diminishment of the other.[41] A third apprehension is that the meaning of justice is so ambiguous, expansive, and elusive that law invariably will be seen as falling short, as failing to meet justice's demands.[42] And here the worry is that law's legitimate authority, such as it is, will be dangerously (and unjustly) eroded.[43] Alternatively, but with consequences no less grave, the impossibility of satisfying justice's demands will eventually be seen as the fault of justice, not of law. On that day, the capacity to resist bad laws in the name of justice will be greatly diminished.

Still other qualms dampen enthusiasm about the possibility of reconnecting law and justice. One of them derives from an understanding of justice as the mediation of the conflicting demands of autonomous, rights-bearing persons.[44] Justice, in this view, is the handmaiden of an arms-length mode of existence and is tonally and affectively uncongenial to the cultivation of genuine community.[45] More generally still, it might be argued that the embrace of legal justice is, at best, a rhetori-

---

self-governance and an increase of both managerial intrusiveness and managerial discretion. The effects on liberty and on law (and legality) are said to be widespread and destructive. Part of what is contended here is that the aspirations of distributive justice are in deep tension with procedural justice.

41. See Roberto M. Unger, *Law and Modern Society* (New York: Free Press, 1977), especially his discussion of the welfare state and the decline of the rule of law, beginning at 193. The potential for conflict between the rule of law and the press of distributive justice is also examined, with more optimistic results than Unger's, by Randy E. Barnett in "Forward: Can Justice and the Rule of Law be Reconciled?" *Harvard Journal of Law & Public Policy* 11 (1988): 622–23. Barnett argues that justice and the rule of law are two ways of coping with "the pervasive social problems of knowledge, interest, and power" (see 622); "[t]he rule of law is neither form for form's sake, nor a second-best approximation of true justice. Rather, the rule of law is what makes possible the knowledge and enforcement of justice in a social setting" (623). Both justice without the rule of law and the rule of law without justice would be "nightmares."

42. The literature is vast on the incompatible expectations that justice creates or purports to impose; perhaps the locus classicus of justice's conflicting claims is John Stuart Mill's catalog at the beginning of chapter 5 in *Utilitarianism*. See Mill, *Utilitarianism*, ed. George Sher (Indianapolis: Hackett Publishing, 1979).

43. For an example, see Tom R. Tyler, *Why People Obey the Law* (New Haven: Yale University Press, 1990). This kind of concern is criticized by Austin Sarat, "Authority, Anxiety, and Procedural Justice: Moving From Scientific Detachment to Critical Engagement," *Law & Society Review* 27 (1993): 647.

44. The (im)possibility of this idea of justice is discussed by Jean Francois Lyotard, *The Differend: Phrases in Dispute* (Minneapolis: University of Minnesota Press, 1988).

45. See Sandel, in *Liberalism and the Limits of Justice;* also, Shklar, in *Faces of Injustice.*

cally appealing device for quieting alarm about the excesses and in-equities social and economic arrangements inevitably arouse.[46] So con-ceived, justice is largely a symbolic response to the incorrigible defects of liberal capitalist societies, not a virtue that these arrangements can promote or make possible.[47]

The fear that legal justice can be put to work in the name of legiti-mating social injustice—for example, by "justifying" outcomes that seem patently, outrageously disproportionate—has been expressed in a different voice, and on different grounds, by Judith Shklar.[48] In *The Faces of Injustice* Shklar argues, inter alia, that the focus on justice inhibits the development of a community that recognizes the culturally constructed quality of boundaries between the ideas of injustice and misfortune and that objects to *passive* injustice as vehemently as it abhors the active vi-olation of rights.[49] But Shklar's dissatisfaction with a narrow concern for justice is pressed even further[50] in her contention that contemporary theory tends almost exclusively to view justice as the "trouser term"[51] and to regard injustice as "simply the absence of justice."[52] In this view, "once we know what is just, we know all we need to know." Shklar writes,

One misses a great deal by looking only at justice. The sense of *in*justice, the difficulties of identifying victims of *in*justice, and the many ways in which we learn to live with each other's *in*justices tend to be ignored, as is the relation of private *in*justice to the pub-lic order.[53] (emphasis added)

46. Douglas Hay, "Property, Authority and the Criminal Law," in *Albion's Fatal Tree,* ed. Douglas Hay, Peter Linebaugh, and E. P. Thompson (Harmondsworth: Penguin, 1975).

47. Marx and Engels present justice in just this light, and Marx, in his "Critique of the Gotha Program," takes essentially the same tack in objecting to "distributive" mea-sures as either necessary or virtuous. See Robert Tucker, ed., *The Marx-Engels Reader,* 2d ed. (New York: W. W. Norton, 1978), 525.

48. Shklar, *Faces of Injustice.*

49. Ibid.

50. Here she is joined, not only by John Stuart Mill in the opening passages of chap-ter 5 in *Utilitarianism,* but also by Elizabeth Wolgast, *The Grammar of Justice* (Ithaca and London: Cornell University Press, 1987), and by A. D. Woozley, "Injustice," *American Philosophical Quarterly,* monograph 7 (1973): 109–22.

51. See J. L. Austin, *How to Do Things with Words* (Cambridge: Harvard University Press, 1975).

52. Shklar, *Faces of Injustice,* 15.

53. Knight, "On the Meaning of Justice," 15.

In Shklar's view, then, we not only lack a full and coherent account of justice, but even if we had one, it would not yield an equally full account of *in*justice, nor would it confront adequately our calloused complacency regarding vast, yet eliminable, misfortunes.

These observations call to mind a variety of uncertainties and ambivalences regarding the relationship of law and justice, but they fall far short of embracing the extreme position that justice be jettisoned from legal discourse. Rather, they remind us of the vastness of our subject, of the difficulty of constructing a single account capable of holding together its many strands, and of the space that exists to theorize anew about justice and injustice in law and legal theory. If progress is to be made, it will be made, we believe, in the kind of detailed examination of specific examples of legal justice or injustice provided by the essays in this book.[54] It will be made by carefully attending to law in history, to the ways law is brought to bear in social life, and to debates about and struggles over particular legal acts. Here emphasizing context, variability, and contingency provides the most promising avenue for scholarship.

As one writer noted recently, "there is no such thing as justice 'in general'; one can meaningfully discuss only fairly concrete injustices and procedures for their mitigation with existing social machinery or possible ways of improving the overall social organization."[55]

Despite the familiar philosophical aspiration for a wholly external, independent and objective standpoint from which to construct a universal account of justice,[56] such an account would be "too abstract to be useful in evaluating actual institutions and practices."[57] To contribute to a fruitful discussion of justice, one must adopt the position, not of knower and author, but of listener.[58] Rational reflection on justice "begins in a hearing" and "in heeding the call." It proceeds by "clarifying the meaning of concepts and issues, describing and explaining social relations, and articulating and defending ideals and principles."[59] The arguments made in the course of this activity are not intended as "defin-

---

54. For a similar argument see Walzer, *Spheres of Justice.*

55. Knight, "On the Meaning of Justice," 15.

56. See Richard Rorty, *Contingency, Irony, and Solidarity* (Cambridge: Cambridge University Press, 1989), chap. 3.

57. Young, *Justice and Difference,* 4.

58. Ibid., citing Jean Francois Lyotard and Jean-Loup Thebaud, *Just Gaming* (Minneapolis: University of Minnesota Press, 1985), 71–72.

59. Young, *Justice and Difference,* 5.

itive demonstration"; rather, "they are addressed to others and await their response in a situated political dialogue."[60] Finally, "(n)ormative reflection must begin from historically specific circumstances because there is nothing but what is, the given, the situated interest in justice, from which to start."[61]

Following Young, the essays in *Justice and Injustice in Law and Legal Theory* all take this "situated" perspective. The way they treat the varying relationships of law and justice neither demands nor issues in an idea of *the* just society in general; rather, the authors allow for "a multitude of conceptions of justice, each derived from the particular conditions of the society and applicable only to them."[62] The defining feature of the conceptions of justice animating these essays is found in their careful attention to "the structural and institutional relations of the society in its totality . . . "[63]

The contributors to the present volume resist any impulse to construct totalizing theories. But even more strikingly, they have written about a variety of legal arrangements—pertaining to speech, nineteenth and early twentieth century immigration law, judicial review, and policing—that substantially determine the overall justness of the state by shaping the normative circumstances and understandings under which citizens live their lives. On this account, justice is less about the distribution of material goods and opportunities, or about particular legal procedures, than it is about the basic institutions of the state and their coherence or incoherence.[64]

---

60. Ibid.

61. Ibid.

62. Iris Young, "Toward A Critical Theory of Justice," *Social Theory and Practice* 7 (1981): 297. Though in her book, Young develops an account of justice that links Habermas's "communicative ethics" with an emphasis on eradicating domination and oppression, she seems to grant that not every theory of justice need have precisely this focus.

63. Ibid., 282.

64. More specifically, several of the essays are studies of various dimensions of voice or significant speech, of who is permitted to speak, about hurtful speech, about the designation of specially authoritative speech, and about the construction of a public voice and its content. The essays thus help us understand how the justice or injustice of law might be assessed from the perspective of a participant (or aspiring participant) in a society that is more or less attuned and committed to giving full and effective voice to its members. Viewed from this perspective, the essays in the present volume point toward a participatory conception of justice which always requires a situated exploration of a legal order's particular self-understandings and arrangements.

For an interesting reflection on the connection between voice and justice, see Mari-

The first essay, Michael Taussig's "The Injustice of Policing: Prehistory and Rectitude," suggests that at the heart of those institutions is a basic contradiction, a tension, between legal justice and violence. It reminds us that there is a vast gap between abstract philosophical arguments about the nature of justice and the institutionalization of legal justice. What fills that gap is the reality of violence. Legal justice without violence is, Taussig contends following Pascal, impotent, but justice in the presence of violence is impossible. Violence is thus essential to, and at the same time destructive of, legal justice. Because it relies on violence, legal justice is always unjust.

Taussig uses Benjamin and Freud to argue that the state and its law are founded in acts of, or the possibility of, violence, and they always are maintained by force. Who, he asks, can really tell the difference between law's justice and its force? In his view the tension between violence and justice, the peculiar combination of might and right that is the law, is exemplified in the practices of policing.

The police, Tassig contends, because they have continuous contact with society's "tabooed" persons, are inevitably contaminated by them. They are corrupted by the corruption to which they must respond. They cannot maintain their innocence while doing the dirty business of coping with crime. Moreover, police corruption is known about and tolerated throughout the legal system. As Tassig notes, this means that a recurring drama of force and fraud is at the heart of law. Policing is always the home of injustice, injustice on which law is dependent even as it denies its dependency. There is after all no one to police those who police the police.

Both Benjamin and Freud tell us that the justice of law can never be pure, that legal justice can be established only through violent acts, and that those acts taint the legal order.[65] Legal justice is bonded to the very injustice it seeks to oppose. Cops and thieves are intertwined; police corruption is the corruption of legal justice itself. The force and fraud that are intrinsic to legal justice are repressed, but never completely. Both surface in bizarre acts wherein the justice of law is overwhelmed by its

anne Constable, "Discussion Outline: Justice and Power in Language and Discourse," (Summer Institute in Sociolegal Studies, Amherst College, 1992, typescript). See also Austin Sarat and Thomas R. Kearns, "Editorial Introduction," in *The Rhetoric of Law*, ed. Austin Sarat and Thomas R. Kearns (Ann Arbor: University of Michigan Press, 1994).

65. For a discussion of this proposition see Austin Sarat and Thomas R. Kearns, eds., *Law's Violence* (Ann Arbor: University of Michigan Press, 1992).

violent underside. As a result, in the realm of legal justice, the "Best you can hope for is a 'minimal level' of badness. . . ."

Robert W. Gordon's "Undoing Historical Injustice" begins, in one sense, where Taussig leaves off. For Gordon, the relationship between law and justice can be apprehended best in those rare historical moments when law responds to what he calls "epochal injustices," namely, the "gross, systemic injustices" perpetrated by previous rulers. Examples of such moments include Federal Reconstruction policy after the Civil War, American antidiscrimination policies in the Second Reconstruction, Allied occupation policy in Germany after World War II, and West German policy toward the newly reunified East German zone. In each of these instances, Gordon claims, we can see how legal institutions both express the relation of society to its history and, at the same time, make the future by redesigning the past. For Gordon, then, the justice or injustice of any legal order can be assessed, at least in part, by the way it writes its own history, the way it narrates the injuries done in its name, and the way it imagines a different future.

Gordon identifies three responses to epochal injustices, which he calls "narrow agency," "broad agency," and "structural approaches." The first focuses on wrongs done by specific perpetrators to specific victims and the second on wrongs done by groups to other groups, while the third seeks to undo injustices by reforming structures. Gordon uses these responses to frame the history of recent debates about legal efforts to remedy racial discrimination in the United States, in particular affirmative action. He demonstrates how people on all sides of those debates appeal to history, with conservatives appealing to historical sources to claim that the history of racial discrimination is irrelevant to present efforts to redress injustices and liberals arguing that historical barriers to racial equality must be demolished.

The view of history deployed by advocates of both the narrow and broad agency models, Gordon contends, is conservative in that it treats past injustices as the isolated acts of bad agents. He prefers, he says, structural explanations and structural approaches because they help us come to terms with the fact that injustice is typically embedded in social systems. Yet he worries that structural explanations and approaches may breed fatalism and despair. Thus, he ends by reminding us that just as there can be no general theory of justice, there can be no theory of how to respond to injustice divorced from the particularities of history and context. It may be, he notes, that "the reformist possibilities of structural understanding may be restricted to societies whose own traditions make plausible a view of history in which good agents can triumph over bad structures."

This insistence on the importance of history and context is carried forward in Nancy F. Cott's essay, "Justice for All? Marriage and Deprivation of Citizenship in the United States." In this essay Cott insists that discussion of legal justice must take into account the way in which allegedly "private" arrangements, such as marriage, have been shaped and affected by public policy. Her particular interest is in the intersection of policies on citizenship and gender justice. The American state, Cott contends, was, during the nineteenth and early twentieth centuries, actively involved in shaping the meaning of women's citizenship through its treatment of cases in which native-born persons married noncitizens. Attending to this treatment shows how a regime formally committed to equality nonetheless could inscribe gender inequality as a basic norm in its laws.

Cott examines an 1855 Act of Congress that afforded citizenship to foreign women who married American men but that did not extend the privilege of citizenship through marriage to American women who married noncitizen men. She also notes the way racial considerations were encoded in this act, since only women who might lawfully be naturalized under then existing law—namely, free, white women—could become citizens through marriage. But lest such policies be seen as the dated vestige of a now repudiated antebellum heritage, Cott notes that under a 1907 Act of Congress, American women who married foreign nationals were deprived of their citizenship. In this way the law regulating citizenship assumed that women's primary political allegiance was to their husbands, not their country. Only with the advent of women's suffrage, and a forty-year-long struggle, was the battle to equalize women's status in the domain of marriage and citizenship completed.

By providing a historical account of the movement from what she regards as injustice perpetrated in the name of the law to legal justice, Cott reminds us of how injustices can be deeply encoded in a legal system and how resistant law can be to the claims of justice. This resistance, Cott argues, occurs because what, in hindsight, appears odious was, in the past, "just the way things had to be." Only when, she says, quoting Thurgood Marshall, "'what once was a "natural" and "self-evident" ordering later comes to be seen as an artificial and invidious constraint on human potential and freedom'" can law move away from injustice toward the realization of a more just society.

Such an effort to break through the "natural" and "self-evident" priority of freedom of speech in the name of gender justice is currently in play in debates about pornography. Joshua Cohen's "Freedom, Equality, Pornography" examines this effort and provides an assessment of the strengths and weaknesses of current arguments about the need to remedy the injustice of women's subordination through legal regulation of pornography. Cohen seeks to explain why progressives—the Left—so frequently oppose antipornography legislation as a response to that injustice. He focuses in particular on the antipornography ordinance drafted and advocated by Catharine MacKinnon and Andrea Dworkin. That ordinance, he contends, is unacceptably broad and intrusive on forms of sexual expression that merit protection. It works new injustices even as it seeks to remedy others.

In Cohen's view, the argument in support of the MacKinnon-Dworkin ordinance is that pornography is a constituent element in the systematic subordination of women, that it contributes to the unjust treatment of persons on the basis of their gender. That is why he puzzles over the Left's reticence to embrace antipornography legislation. This reticence, Cohen suggests, is attributable to the pull of a competing commitment, a commitment to expressive freedom. This commitment stands against the Left's desire to use law to remedy social injustice. Cohen identifies three interests—expressive, deliberative, and informational—the protection of which require resistance to the most stringent antipornography regulations. While he believes that some form of regulation might be appropriate, his analysis of the contemporary context in which such a law might be drafted leads him to call for an effort to "attack the injustice of inequality and subordination while accommodating the importance of pleasure."

The debate about pornography is, along with the debate about abortion, one of the most hotly contested legal issues in the United States. They are issues, as we have seen, in which the justice claims are strong, but in which resistance to legal intervention is equally strong. The movement from pornography to abortion provides the vehicle through which Frank Michelman, in the last essay in this volume, examines the justness of what he calls "judicial supremacy." Judicial supremacy is, as Michelman sees it, the practice of giving independent judges final authority over "questions of constitutional-legal meaning

... that in kind and degree goes quite beyond what is required for the arbitral function of the law. . . ." Abortion is, for him, a classic instance in which the courts have exercised such authority and, in so doing, have decided major questions of political morality.

Michelman analyzes Ronald Dworkin's defense of judicial supremacy, a defense most powerfully articulated in the context of abortion rights, and asks whether a persuasive case can be made for the justness of this particular institutional practice. Dworkin, Michelman argues, defends judicial supremacy as a practice conceptually embedded in the liberal ideal of government under law. But he suggests, contrary to Dworkin, that it is neither a logical entailment of justice nor a requisite of the rule of law. In his view, popularly based determination of constitutional questions would be as viable as judicial supremacy.

In addition, Michelman turns Dworkin's eloquent arguments in favor of a responsibility-based political morality, in which rights protect the unique human capacity for self-creation, into an argument *for* including citizens in the processes of judgment through which meaning is given to law. On Dworkin's own terms, which Michelman argues are prudential and consequentialist, as well as on the grounds of a dignitary and participatory conception of justice itself, judicial supremacy must be rejected. It neither assuredly advances the cause of justice in particular cases nor cultivates the capacity of citizens to rise to the demands of justice in their own political lives.

From Taussig to Michelman, from the dilemmas of policing to the routines of judicial review, the claims justice makes on law are powerful, yet the vindication of justice through law is by no means certain. Only by attending to context, history, and contingency can we understand, most often in retrospect, why, on this occasion or that, law was the ally of injustice and the adversary of justice. Only by suspending the rituals of philosophical abstraction can scholars identify the conditions under which law heeds the call of justice. Only by doing so can scholarship help promote a more just legality.

The Injustice of Policing: Prehistory and Rectitude

Michael Taussig

Gewalt, f.(-en) power, authority, dominion, might, force, violence.

This chapter concerns policing democracy, and if I appear to draw excessively on fantasies, images, and exotic worlds of violence and transformation, it is not because I want to downplay the awesome solidity of the police, but because it is there, in the fantasies, that I discern a more pressing need for thinking on this matter—in a sort of spin-off of what the novelist J. M. Coetzee, in a story about CIA activity in the Vietnam War, referred to as "mythological warfare."[1] Yet my subject is more difficult in that we do not at first think in terms of war in foreign lands where the exotic and the horrific loom large when we think of the police—"our police," as we are wont to say. Nevertheless, Coetzee has a point long overdue when it comes to our police; only here, despite their being so close to home, I wish to draw attention not to their full-bodied proximity but to their ability to slip away, to the mythological warfare of decorporealization referred to by Walter Benjamin in his "Critique of Violence" as their ghostly being, a suspended sort of violent nothingness.[2]

Let me put it this way (noting that "violence" here is a very one-sided translation of the term used by Benjamin, namely *Gewalt,* mean-

---

1. J. M. Coetzee,"The Vietnam Project," in *Dusklands* (Harmondsworth: Penguin Books, 1974), 1–49.
2. Walter Benjamin, "Zur Kritik der Gewalt," translated as "Critique of Violence," in *Reflections,* ed. Peter Demetz (New York: Harcourt Brace Jovanovich, 1978), 277–301, at 286–87. First published in 1920–21.

ing both violence *and* authority): the ghostliness of the police is not because they abuse their power, but that this power cannot be anything
else but corrupt because of the specific way it combines might with
right. The "law" of the police, notes Benjamin, is independent of the rest
of the law. It "really marks the point at which the state, whether from
impotence or because of the immanent connections within any legal system, can no longer guarantee through the legal system the empirical
ends it desires at any price to attain."[3] Thus, no matter how much moral
imperative dictates weeding out corruption among the police, intelligence decrees that one approach this with a certain pessimism, understanding the task as endless, if not forlorn, in its necessity. Such an approach puts the task of the critic, legal or literary, as in "Critique of
Gewalt," in a difficult and even dubious light, criticism itself being close
cousin to policing. Mindful of that, then, we can see that such a critique
amounts to a policing of policing, a theoretical forerunner to what has
now been instituted for the first time in modern history, and long after
Benjamin's time, as human rights organizations. Apart from its focus on
philosophy and theology, its theoretical sophistication, and its passion
for social revolution, what distinguishes Benjamin from such organizations, however, as from liberalism in general, is the clear recognition that
the police are not and never can be subject to law.[4] What, then, are they
subject to? Mythological warfare begins to take on unsuspected characteristics when hauled back from wars executed in poor, third world
countries.

This becomes somewhat clearer if we realize it is a waste of time
trying to define the characteristics of policing in itself "before" or outside of "corruption," for it is my central claim here that corruption
comes first and sets the decisive parameters such that policing *is* a form
of corruption. Instead of trying to think of an island of purity, namely
the police, with some hidden portals for the entry of evil from the outside—a "few rotten apples" destroying the whole barrel, as they say—
or of an original innocence fatefully besmirched by the Fall after the contact with crime, we should rather see policing as that enigmatic power
arising from its immersion in and constant contact with contagion, with
the tabooed, thus partaking of the properties of corruption itself.

---

3. Ibid., 287.
4. He writes that the police are suspended from both the law-making and law-founding forms of violence.

"Tough Cops, Not Brutal Cops," appeals a recent *New York Times* editorial that, in trying to slice through this Gordian knot and separate toughness from brutality, finds itself tying still more knots and reduced to pious finger wagging. The police commissioner of New York is cited as saying that "police officers are 'between a rock and hard place' because there is no way they can attempt to reclaim drug-ridden neighborhoods without being tough." "True," continues the editorial writer. "But as the Commissioner also notes, there is a 'right way to do it and a wrong way to do it' [and] no police officer worthy of his or her shield can fail to know the difference between aggressive policing and brutality."[5] Here the text ends: anybody worth the shield can tell the difference—the difference between aggressive policing and brutality. Could there be a more enigmatic—or for that matter, brutal—ending? It could in fact end anywhere, for it comes out of nowhere and goes back into nowhere, coursing the thin blue line of a Möbius strip of injunction and despair. Unable to define what the difference between aggressive policing and brutality is, the text "ends" with moralistic finger wagging invoking strange deities—the medieval evocation of the honor of the shield—meaning the shield-shaped police badge. Mythological warfare seems close to the surface here because it is only through force compressed into moralizing vapor, the finger waving back and forth between that rock and that hard place, that the desired distinction between toughness and brutality can and will be upheld.

One remembers the recent scene at the thirtieth precinct in northwest Harlem, New York City, where the police accused of corruption had their badges solemnly removed by the commissioner in a deft enactment of castration and beheading. One remembers George Nova who, ever since he was a little boy, so they say, wanted to be a cop. Here was a superb police officer. "It's mind-boggling how someone could be so good. He just had the knack," said a supervisor at the thirtieth precinct. Nova had an uncanny sense of crime. But at the same time, now it is revealed, he turns out to have been the most crooked of the lot. The best was the worst. Such are the ways of policing. Be it noted that throughout his brilliant career, until apprehended, he had but one "command discipline," a minor infraction—lending his shield to a friend to

---

5. Editorial, *New York Times*, 5 May 1994, A26.

use with a Halloween costume.[6] Then one remembers not the policeman who became a thief but the thief who became a saint, Saint Genet, at the bar crushed by Bernadino's huskiness and self-assurance: "I was excited chiefly by the invisible presence of his inspector's badge. The metal object had for me the power of a cigarette lighter in the fingers of a workman, or the buckle of an army belt, of a switchblade, of a caliper, objects in which the quality of males is violently concentrated. Had I been alone with him in a dark corner, I might have been bold enough to graze the cloth, to slip my hand under the lapel where cops usually wear the badge, and I would have trembled just as if I had been opening his fly."[7]

At first it seems paradoxical that this thief could be so enamored of cops, their badge and their dicks. But maybe that's the point—the straining of contradiction, the what-we-all-know-anyway. It's not that cops are thieves, too. No! I insist on the difference! If they're thieves, then they're "cop-thieves." It's that cops and thieves are erotically intertwined and that the thin blue line separating them is more like a veil in a striptease. Perhaps it's bad sex, when all is said and done, and perhaps Genet has a problem here, but that's another discussion. What should hold us are the curious properties of the distinction *uniting* the criminal to the policeman.

"All's fair in love and war," goes the saying, and with it would seem to go much of the law as well, not because of the approval of abandon but because of the indirect wisdom in proverbs, that love and enmity are, through the law of *unfairness*, tightly interlocked.[8] A recent *New Yorker* essay on the U.S. attorney's office for northern Illinois and its prosecution of the Blackstone Rangers brings out this idea in a startling manner. Drawing attention to a so-called "modern" trend in law enforcement toward prosecution of entire criminal organizations such as gangs and Mafia families in place of individuals, the article notes that this trend relies heavily on an alliance between prosecutors and turncoats from such organizations. Fraught with hazards, however, the greatest danger to such reliance "is not that what seems to be polar opposites—prosecutors and criminals—might never find a way to work

6. N. R. Kleinfield and James McKinley Jr., "Lives of Courage and Sacrifices, Corruption and Betrayals in Blue," *New York Times*, 25 April 1994, B4.

7. Jean Genet, *The Thief's Journal* (Harmondsworth: Penguin, 1976), 157.

8. On the wisdom of proverbs, see the striking essay by Jean Paulhan "Sacred Language," pp. 304–21, in *The College of Sociology*, ed. Denis Hollier (Minneapolis: University of Minnesota Press, 1988).

together," maintains the author. "Rather it is just the reverse—that the good guys and the bad guys may fall in love."[9]

Now, "falling in love" is one of those metaphorically capacious expressions perfect for the quintessentially theatrical world of cops and crims—"good guys and bad guys"—where passion no less than ambivalence oozes from every pore. To fall—from the heights of law, for instance, from self-control, for instance, into the pit, into the desires of the criminal, into unholiness—is here preordained as in ancient mythology despite the "modernity" of it all, fax machines, automatic weapons, and tape recorders included. At one point a tape recording was secretly made in what we now see as the "classic" and predictable move, the police policing the police, of a telephone call between the chief prosecutor's assistant and one of the "turncoats" in jail. The tape was played in court as evidence against the prosecutor. It was, to say the least, embarrassing: a matter of phone sex on the line between the U.S. government's prosecutor's office in downtown Chicago and the Metropolitan Correctional Center and nobody able to say who was sexing whom, the prosecutor's assistant or the admitted murderer.

> She laughed. "Ten minutes in a locked room. That's all it would take."
> "All right, Rindy," Hunter said, changing the subject. "We done had enough business for the day. You have to tell me bedtime stories for the night."
> "Tell you a bed time story? Gee."
> "Yeah, I have tension, too. You know."
> "You poor thing."
> "And you help me release my tension."
> "I don't know, Eugene," Luchetta said. "Oh, let me see, what kind of story can I tell you . . . What would you have me do first?"
> "I just want to look."
> "Look but don't touch," Luchetta said. "I don't think so."[10]

And so it went on, in gathering waves of telephonic tumescence binding captor to prisoner, prosecutor to murderer cum informant.

The courtroom was very quiet when this tape was played. "Actu-

---

9. Jeffrey Toobin, "Capone's Revenge," *New Yorker*, 23 May 1994, 46–59, at 47.
10. Ibid., 55.

ally," comments the author, "it is not clear precisely what rule if any was broken by this conversation . . . It was inappropriate, bizarre, and embarrassing, but not, perhaps, illegal." And this surely, is Benjamin's point? The murky absence of precision in policing, combined with the spectral (read erotic) effect of such, as herewith demonstrated, is reinforced by the author's further choice of figurative language with his surmise that, for the presiding judge, this taped conversation must have been the last straw, the final and clear indication that the prosecution and the criminals had "ceased operating at some distance from one another and that their alliance was an unholy one."[11] Genet would be the first to testify to the inherent necessity, let alone unholiness, of this alliance.

No less potentially spectral, if not erotic, is the distinction between the cops and the courts, policing in the rough and tumble of the streets, on one side, and the calm adjudication of justice before the bench, on the other. Where does one end and the other begin? Where does the law of force give way to the force of law? What is one to make of the "emperor's new clothes" type of situation of the public secret that judges and prosecutors, in New York City for instance, give tacit approval to cops perjuring themselves in court? The head of the city's Legal Aid criminal division is cited recently as saying that "the police regularly invent witnesses, tailor their testimony to meet constitutional objections, and alter arrest records." What's more, "prosecutors and judges wink at it."[12]

Theatrical performance is crucial to the success of this public secret, which sets the stage for the recurring drama of force and fraud at the heart of the system of justice. The courtroom serves merely as the play within the play. As was said at the trial for perjury of a police officer, John Rossi, who beat up a prisoner named Luis Mora so as to force a false confession that would exonerate the officer from having committed a minor infraction: "This perjury is monstrous because the lie seems like the truth. Luis Mora looked guilty to John Rossi. He dressed guilty. He had a record of guilt. Luis Mora is the perfect fall guy. John Rossi knew after all those years of working with assistant district attorneys, of testifying before a grand jury, testifying before judges, that he would have no trouble selling a guy like Luis Mora up the river."[13] But to the

11. Ibid., 56.
12. Robert Baum as cited by Joe Sexton, "Testilying," *New York Times*, 4 May 1994, 26.
13. Ibid., 26.

police community, the prosecution of Officer Rossi was "wrongheaded and overzealous." It failed to take into account the dangers and difficulties of policing.

Strangest of all, to Officer Rossi it didn't seem to have happened at all. He didn't even believe the case had been brought against him. "From the second I realized they were going to prosecute me to this second right now," he said after the case had been heard and he'd been sentenced, "it's been beyond me. It seems fictional."[14]

And well he might dazedly wonder at the fictional quality at work on his fictions. After all, an attorney writing a month before this news report stated that in her sixteen years working in the city she had neither seen nor heard of a New York City prosecutor bringing a cop to court for perjury. What's more, she says that while it's routine in court to hear police give evidence that would strain the credulity of a seven-year-old, judges rarely reject such testimony as false.[15]

But is it not the very same system that lets us know of its corruption? And is that not its saving grace? But what then if these confessions change nothing, as seems likely? More than likely.

Is this then the ultimate theater, confessions and commissions of inquiry, witnesses in black ski masks and a whole supporting cast performing a public ritual of purgation undertaken with each new mayor or every decade, a forced confession to the gods of the city? Farewell to the land of absolutes no less than absolution; the best you can hope for is a "minimal level" of badness achieved through frequent and regular reamings, like cleaning the toilet bowl. Is this the ultimate sign of the divine, revealing how scarce, indeed how miraculous, justice is?

Force and fraud. Theater. Theaters of operation. Mythological warfare. Vietnam. Myths are bold, the characters larger than life. Two policemen rode the patrol car cruising the thirtieth precinct in northwest Harlem. The report read that "a drug crazed individual" was firing at another man. The two policemen "scrambled" out of their cars as other drug dealers joined in. "It was like Vietnam out there," a police officer said. Officer Vasquez shot one man down but as he was reloading, the downed man staggered to his knees, despite severe wounds, aiming his gun at Vasquez. Without hesitation Vasquez's partner, Jorge Alvarez,

14. Ibid.
15. Jane B. Freidson, Letter to the Editor, New York Times, 6 May 1994. Also see letter of rebuttal by H. Morgenthau, of her allegation that police are not prosecuted for perjury, New York Times, 13 May 1994.

dived in front of him and killed the would-be killer. A few months later, as in a Greek tragedy, Alvarez turned in his partner for corruption as a way of mitigating his own involvement in crime. Yes! Maybe it was like Vietnam "out there." Alvarez's heroism haunted the minds of the other officers. "You have to look back and wonder whether Jorge did Vasquez a favor or not," commented one officer. "Maybe the best thing would have been if Vasquez had died right there. He would have been a hero. His family would have received a pension. Now his family is disgraced. The man is looking at life in prison. Who would want to be him?" Investigators policing the police "remain uncertain of just when and why any went bad." It is pointed out that the best cover is to do your job not just well but extremely well. The best way to be the worst is to be the best. The report speaks of cops "being like the beach"—subject to continuous erosion by the temptations thrown their way by crime.[16] This beats Kafka. You can see the waves pounding in from the surging sea, waves of money, waves of drugs, waves of secrets rolling in from the polluted ocean that has no beginning and no end.

The report speaks of men "unraveling," overwhelmed by the size of the monthly mortgage payments; the unpaid taxes; the Datsun they own with over 200,000 miles on it; the house foreclosed; separations, sometimes divorces; the deprived "backgrounds." Then there are the brown paper bags picked up at the bodega with tens of thousands of dollars. Who could resist? But would any of that explain diving in front of your partner to save his life? The drama is plain and absorbing: honest men slowly sucked into not just crime but treason—after all, they are police! For them to stoop to crime is to double the crime. Not thieves, but "cop-thieves," double-men. The great art of transformation: might there not be seduction in just that? Is this not Genet's pleasure of betrayal, combining the murder of the (Law of the) Father and then of the brother-accomplice, the "eternal return" of the first of the great transgressions on the way to sanctity? The ultimate in oedipal bravado. And the report speaks of gaining a partial understanding of "the road to the dark side of the law." We stand appalled—yet perhaps also a little excited—by the horrendous inevitability invoked by the notion here of a "road" to the storming depths. What road is this? Spellbound by the human drama, however, the report fails to follow up on this insight—that

---

16. Kleinfield and McKinley, "Lives of Courage," B4.

the law itself no less than human beings depends on, yet must deny, this "dark side" as part of its very being.

As policing recedes into the pit of "darkness," into the underworld that claims it, heart and soul, so it creates a hierarchy of invisible layers of other police—perhaps "better" and more "noble" police—whose function it is to police the police. Note the time-honored practice of using a thief to catch a thief as with the now routine practice of "the wire" in which a cop is wired to a tape recorder by a tiny microphone, like an animal of prey, trapping a fellow cop into an incriminating chat at the Policeman's Benevolent Society's barbecue. This practice has led to the further practice of police now secretly wearing wire detectors available at "spy shops" in New York City. Let us not forget the role of the FBI in conducting "sting" operations with patience and guile over many months, involving (once again) these notorious brown paper bags with $10,000 in them on kitchen countertops under the surveillance of a hidden video camera set to capture the police who are unable to resist the bait as they search apartments for drugs. All of which leads to other questions concerning mythological warfare, which, as with spy thrillers in art and real life, entails worlds within worlds of mutual suspicion, disguise, and deception. Can the law be dependent on something as fluid and eerie as policing through infinite regress? Who polices the police policing the police? It's like the shamans as Plato describes them in Ion, as I discerned them in the southwest of Colombia, each one dependent on a more powerful one—and the one at the end, at the headwaters of the river lost in the forest, what would he look like? What language would he speak? Who could he turn to in his moments of insight and weakness? It's said that the (in)famous head of the FBI J. Edgar Hoover had thirty-five file drawers and six filing cabinets that nobody but his personal secretary had access to, with dirt on presidents and important politicians and officials (including FBI officials). Is that the end point? When he died it caused a panic. His secretary, Helen Gandy, had to hide the files in Hoover's home and then destroyed an unspecified number of them. But did she destroy all? And why is this mysterious lode of dirt on the rich and powerful referred to sometimes as "gold" and other times as "a bucket of worms"?[17]

But the most intriguing sign of the theater of visibility and invisi-

---

17. Curt Gentry, *J. Edgar Hoover: The Man and the Secrets* (New York: Norton, 1991), 728–30.

bility is the frequent attention paid in the press to the off-duty cop out of uniform who apprehends a criminal—as in a hairdressing salon or in a speeding car. These stories never fail to impress me although I am not sure why. Is it because that policing—as with the ministry of religion, or a medical doctor, for instance—is more than just a job, so that even off duty one is still on duty? Is it because you are made suddenly to realize that you never know if the person beside you is an off-duty cop and that the line between the police and the public is not uniformly well defined when all along you thought it was and should be? Is it because there is something almost supernatural and certainly Hollywoodesque about the quicksilver transformation from the Clark Kent figure into the Superman? Or is it because of the joy one feels that the tables were so unexpectedly turned on a criminal unexpectedly taking advantage of an unsuspecting public?

Here I cannot stop from wondering about the rather pathetic displays of rebellion involved in my switching back and forth from *police* to *cop*. This word *cop*, no less than *police*, seems to have the wondrous ambivalent power of those strange "primal" words that Freud brought to our attention.[18] But the term *cop* is doubly curious in that as the underside or left-handed term, not only does it have its official counterpart in *police*, but it itself has crept into if not the official then certainly the quasi-official and respectable U.S. lexicon. Its usage conveys not only critical distance from the "police" but a peculiar mix of insult and endearment, and much the same applies to the litany of cop appellations such as *dick, fuzz, flatfoot, sleuth, gumshoe* and so forth. The folkloric observation of one facet of policing, the performance of the "good cop, bad cop" routine, speaks eloquently to such manifestations of ambivalence. It is more than testimony to the fact that policing so easily lends itself to theatrical representation, and it is more than testimony to the way corruption defines policing in which the threat posed by the "bad cop" is even less important than the shocking duplicity of the "good cop." It is also testimony to the quasi-sacred ambivalence of an authority whose corruption manifests a specific constellation of attraction and equally great repulsion.[19] Let us emphasize at this point, therefore, Freud's ren-

---

18. Sigmund Freud, "The Antithetical Meaning of Primal Words," *The Standard Edition of the Complete Psychological Works of Sigmund Freud*, vol. 11 (London: Hogarth, 1957), 153–61.

19. Cf. Georges Bataille's work on the sacred, the abject, and power as in "Attraction and Repulsion II" in *The College of Sociology: 1937–39*, ed. Denis Hollier (Minneapolis: Uni-

dition of extant ethnography and classical reference where he noted the following salient features of the taboo. "The meaning of 'taboo,' as we see it," he wrote (in 1913), "diverges in two contrary directions. To us it means, on the one hand, 'sacred,' 'consecrated,' and on the other 'uncanny,' 'dangerous,' 'forbidden,' 'unclean.'" Moreover, contact with the tabooed person or object, he noted (as the strangest fact of all), leads to contagion by the same power such that that person in turn acquires the property of being tabooed.[20]

Taboo and the Phobic Object

It is this quasi-sacred purity and impurity of policing that seem to me to underlie Benjamin's figure of ghosts haunting not traditional but modern societies. Their power is formless, Benjamin wrote of the police, like their "nowhere tangible, all-pervasive, ghostly presence in the life of civilized states." This haunting presence is all the more marked, he noted, in democracies as compared with authoritarian states and monarchies.[21]

Centrally concerned in 1920 in an age of revolution and counter-revolution with the implications violence holds for reason, no less than for law, Benjamin (aged all of 28) strove to define rights of violence—as in the proletarian general strike, and with what he called the "divine justice of destruction," which was opposed to the "mythic violence that founds law."[22] He was especially interested in phenomena destabilizing the boundary between might and right (which is, of course, the grotesque beauty of the word "Gewalt"), and he singled out capital punishment, for instance, as that act of law preservation which, through its

---

versity of Minnesota Press, 1988), 113–24; and in Bataille, *The Accursed Share*, 2 vols. (New York: Zone Books, 1988, 1991). Also Roger Caillois, "Power," in Hollier's *College of Sociology*, 125–36. This last essay seems to be a composite Bataille-Caillois product.

20. Sigmund Freud, *The Standard Edition of the Complete Psychological Works of Sigmund Freud*. Vol. 13, *Totem and Taboo* (London: Hogarth, 1957), 1–161 at 18, 22.

21. Benjamin, "Critique of Violence," 287.

22. Of importance here was Georges Sorel's eclectic and fascinating work, *Reflections on Violence*, first published in 1915. Sorel has separate chapters on "The Proletarian Strike" and "The Political General Strike." His disposition to see "the big picture," to see violence no less than the general strike in terms of apocalyptic Christian mythology, makes this essay germane to Benjamin's similarly philosophical and religious concerns with violence. Furthermore, it seems to me that this work of Sorel's is the basis to Benjamin's strange gestures toward "pessimism" at the end of the latter's essay on surrealism—a pessimism that fuses eloquently with Benjamin's refiguration of Blanqui.

exercising the highest violence possible within the legal system, the power over life and death, irresistibly brings forth the violent origins of law at the same time as it acts to maintain law and hence reveals what he called "rottenness" within the law. Such rottenness entails mystifications separating no less than joining violence to reason—nowhere more so than in the role fulfilled by the police who, through violence or the threat of violence, daily *make* law as much as they maintain it. Policing goes beyond the "rottenness" implicated by capital punishment, to what Benjamin sees as "ignominy," a "far more unnatural [monstrous, *widernaturlichern*] combination" of law-preserving and law-founding violence.

This unabashed disgust exhibited by Benjamin toward our boys in blue strikes me as strange in what is otherwise an essay remarkable for its lofty and somber tone poised on the edge of an incantation. It's as if the mixture of categories upsets him more than the violent reality it is meant to illuminate. Hence, in his attempts to pin down what is at the core of policing, he uses a variety of terms in quick succession, moving from the *rottenness* within the law as revealed by capital punishment to the far more *unnatural and monstrous combination,* the *spectral mixture,* the *ignominy* that arises from the *suspension of the separation,* and finally to the *emancipation* from conditions of both law making and law maintaining.[23]

What then binds "rottenness" and "monstrous combinations" to "spectrality"? And if it is this magnified rottenness that accounts in some way for the spectral nature of policing haunting democratic states, then it not only behooves us to consider to what degree and in what ways the violence founding law in any particular society may continue to "inhabit" contemporary law keeping, but what else this monstrosity might signify other than the "monstrous combination" of ends and means, law-making and law-maintaining, that Benjamin belabors.

Here Benjamin's effort to theologically frame the discussion of police violence in democracies can be restaged by inquiring, along with Bataille and Caillois, into the sacred sociology of taboo and transgression, it being understood that the spectral nature of police is due *not to unclear boundaries but to the incessant demand for transgression by the boundary itself.*[24] Let us not forget that it's the police who "man" this thin blue

---

23. Benjamin, "Critique of Violence," 286.

24. Bataille, see note 19. Roger Caillois, "The Sociology of the Executioner," in *The College of Sociology: 1937–39,* ed. Denis Hollier (Minneapolis: University of Minnesota

line. In the final analysis—but of course there never is one—the ethnography is clear: for the police, life is a beach.

Prehistory and Rectitude

Between earth and water, the beach is the prehistoric zone where life began. This prehistoricity—so Benjamin could be seen as arguing in his essay on Kafka[25]—is reactivated by the modern state, and the police are foremost in this primordial endeavor. Where might this put Thomas Hobbes' theory of power, Hobbes the materialist, with his mystical theory of the "awe" intrinsic to that infamous sword "without which covenants are but words"? Where does this put Leviathan, crawling out of the mud onto the very same beach?

The sword, which upholds the power of words, lies *outside* the circle of words. It's "meaning" draws on quite other realms of reference and bodies of feeling. These are not easy to talk about. Words are lacking. In this very otherness in the object world of bodies and weapons, the awe of Hobbes' sword allows for the mystical perfection of Leviathan—the point being that the awe, as the force necessary for law, is a mystical product of *defilement*; the radiance created when the aloof nobility of the law stoops to brutality. This is the movement. The moment. Leviathan, that mortal god, is a monster, after all, the great enemy of God, whose sublime status rests upon the metamorphosis of brutality into sacred force.

Added to this sacred quality of brutality is the sheer inexplicability that *must* define terror—especially the terror that underpins reason as a world historical mythological movement. Consider the prevalence and importance of violence to which Benjamin's essay alerts us in the law-founding acts and mythologies of modern states. We have already hinted at Freud's allegory of patricide at the formation of (the incest) taboo and Law, but let us note also the law-founding violence—as represented—in the Great Bourgeois as much as the Great Communist revolutions. Consider also the violence in so many of the Great Anti-

---

Press, 1988). This proviso—emphasizing not the blurring but the need set up by the boundary for its transgression sets this analysis poles apart philosophically and sociologically from the approach to taboo and contagion developed by Mary Douglas in her work on purity and danger.

25. Walter Benjamin, "Franz Kafka: On The Tenth Anniversary of His Death," in *Illuminations*, ed. Hannah Arendt (New York: Schocken, 1969), 111–40.

Colonial Struggles. Finally, consider these Western mythologies; the expulsion from the Garden of Eden; the violence necessary to "rescue" the enchained in Plato's cave dragging them kicking and screaming to the beauty of the sun's fiery light and therewith the founding of the Republic based on pure Law; Hegel's mysterious violence that out of nowhere kicks off the phenomenology with the life and death struggle of master and slave—"Therefore," writes Kojeve with reference to the phonomenology, "to speak of the 'origin' of Self-Consciousness it is necessary to speak of a fight to the death for 'recognition.'" In this scheme "it is in the Terror that the State is realized."[26]

What is so unnerving with all this is that the terror itself usually lies resolutely beyond analysis. It is a given, an absolute of some sort, where explanation ceases. It belongs to the gods. (And we take note that in many of these instances, it is the terror that paves the way for the rule of reason.)

In a move that coincided with a general shift of interest in social science toward culture and symbols, Louis Althusser turned what he considered a vulgar marxism on its head, teaching that the state was a cultural force and not simply a "body of armed men." Yet what seems overlooked here is precisely the culture of armed men, meaning the culture of force, brute force and uncontained violence *with meaning none other than itself.*[27] Althusser's break into culture was predicated on what now must surely seem a woefully impoverished vision of culture as a constraining, external, force of ritual that he also called "material practises," but it was one of his students, Nicos Poulantzas who, not too long before killing himself, set forth the theatrical nature of state violence, thus combining the "materialism" of his master, at least as regards the human body and the technology of weapons, with the fantastic—theatrical—figures and emotional surges accompanying violence. It was like a confession as to a vague something that had always been present, yet denied, in that vast system of modern sociology and political theory but that now, thanks to an appreciation of statecraft as stagecraft, announced its untoward self. "Repression," he wrote, "is never pure negativity, and it is not exhausted either in the actual exercise of physical

---

26. Alexander Kojeve, *Introduction to the Reading of Hegel,* ed. Alan Bloom (Ithaca: Cornell University Press, 1980), 7.

27. Louis Althusser, *Lenin and Philosophy, And Other Essays,* trans. Ben Brewster (New York: Monthly Review, 1971). Widely read and cited for a decade or more in this collection was the essay "Ideology and Ideological State Apparatuses," 127–86.

violence or in its internalization. There is something else to repression, something about which people seldom talk; namely the mechanisms of fear." I have referred to these mechanisms, he continues, "as the theatricals of that truly Kafkaesque castle of the modern state. They are inscribed in the labyrinths where modern law becomes a practical reality."[28]

What is fascinating is the lack of talk that Poulantzas strives to talk to, and what such silence concerning the mechanisms of fear implies with regards to the theatrical power of the castle as, with alarming vigor, the call goes out today as I write, here, in New York, as elsewhere, for more police, more prisons, and more capital punishment. For where the silence finds an outlet is in that decidedly Other theater, the "negative sacred" fantasy-theater par excellence of the underworld, the mafia, the street gangs, the paramilitary, the crack dealers, the child abusers, the Oklahoma bombing . . . as a mirror image of the Castle of State, a dark unseemly hell-place of violently disposed not just criminal but evil persons on whose desperate image the Castle sustains itself. And while the theater of the Castle needs this other theater, and vice versa, such that the mystical powers of the one are transformed into the mystical powers of the other, it would seem that it is always the negative sacred—hell and the underworld—that provide the most compelling scenarios and performative power for the mystical foundations of authority and this is why the fear that *can* be spoken is displaced Elsewhere—onto the black man on death row, for instance, and the mysterious brotherhood of the National Rifle Association. Waco, Texas is merely one of the most recent instances and what catches at the heart with Waco is not so much the craziness of the religious zealots but the window they opened onto the spectacular mythology of the Law providing a vivid performance of fraud and catastrophe. Who could believe these blood curdling police no less absurd than bizarre, even existed, *Alcohol, Tobacco, and Firearms*, enlisted by rumors of Armageddon? From what portcullis of the Castle did they emerge?

Benjamin felt that the prehistoricity of the state-world in Kafka was incomparably older than the world of myth and that redemption—for we cannot conclude these pessimistic ruminations on the inevitability of corruption without at least a nod in that direction—could be imag-

---

28. Nicos Poulantzas, *State, Power, Socialism*, trans. Patrick Camiller (New Left Books: London, 1978), 83.

ined, if not sought, between myth and fairy tale. And surely it is the living theater of kitsch where the mythology of the sacred, pure or evil, is suddenly evacuated from policing and the three stooges take over as in Kafka's trial in the always possible comic displacement of the tragic that is crime. The truly corrupt policeman is not the one who, beach-like, is eroded by the waves of crime washing over him. Rather, he is the one who maladroitly stands in the way of the smooth functioning of the taboo and instead of allowing free passage for the conversion of crime into righteousness, lends his badge for a Halloween party.

Undoing Historical Injustice

Robert W. Gordon

My subject in this chapter is that of legal responses of liberal polities to epochal injustices. A regime comes to power—whether by conquest and occupation, by violent revolution, or by peaceful transition does not matter for the present—in a society whose previous rulers and people have practiced or permitted what the new regime judges to have been gross, systemic injustices. The legal responses chosen by the regime express a relation of the new society with its history, how legal systems try to make the future by redesigning the past and their connection with it. Most of my examples will come from four cases I have been trying to understand in detail: U.S. Federal Reconstruction policy after the Civil War; American anti-race-discrimination policies in the Second Reconstruction, focusing on affirmative action; Allied occupation policy in the American zone of Germany after World War II; and, briefly and in passing, the policies being debated and adopted by postcommunist regimes in Germany and Eastern Europe to deal with their communist pasts.

Each type of response comes embedded in a history, a narrative that stitches together the society's past and future. In that narrative the period of injustice usually figures as a deviation from, or a distortion of, the history that should have happened instead—a departure from the society's traditional norms and practices or from some trajectory of evo-

This essay is in memory of Alan Freeman, a piercing analyst of structural injustice. It is a revised and expanded version of a lecture given at Amherst College on March 8, 1994. Comments at the Amherst lecture, at a meeting of the University of Chicago's seminar on Comparative Legal History in April 1994 (especially those of Julius Kirshner, who began by asking, "What do you mean by 'justice', anyway?"), and of Owen Fiss, Ariela Gross, Thomas Heller, and Sophie Pirie in conversation, have helped me grope toward what I was trying to say. I want to acknowledge the admirable research assistance of Ariela Gross, without which I would never have gotten this far.

lutionary development that the society had previously followed or, alternatively, should have been following. When injustice is portrayed as a deviation from a counterfactual history—traditional, evolutionary, or even utopian—the regime's response to injustice is a way of defining the new society's identity by reweaving the severed threads of memory—or to vary the metaphor, by getting history back on track. To put this another way, every legal proposal to undo injustice comes with a story attached explaining what went wrong and how to reconnect to the normal and normatively acceptable path.

Indeed one way we commonly—though, as I'll argue, very misleadingly—classify modes of response to injustice is expressly in terms of relation to the past—as either backward looking or forward looking. I'm thinking of the familiar distinctions between justice and policy, adjudication and administration, righting of past wrongs and prevention of new ones, corrective compensation and social engineering. Such distinctions have been salient in debates in the context of arguments over the proper scope of judicial activism, whether courts are appropriate and capable agents to undertake social policy-making through the mechanisms and remedies of "public law litigation," the class action, and structural injunction.[1]

Let me suggest a somewhat different set of categories: I'll call these narrow agency, broad agency, and structural approaches to injustice. As the names suggest, they attribute injustice, respectively, to bad actors, bad groups, and bad structures.

1. The *narrow-agency* framing of injustice is as wrongs done by specific perpetrators to specific victims; the remedy is the limited and negative retributive sanction of the criminal process or the corrective remedy of the civil suit for compensatory damages. By these means the world is restored to normal by the exaction of an equivalence for the wrong done, the harm inflicted.

2. *Broad-agency* approaches aim at corrective or compensatory justice extended from individuals to collectivities—groups and entities: many wrongs have been done, by collective perpetrators to collective victims. Sometimes of course the agency paradigm can be stretched to accommodate broad-agency theories of liability and remedy in courts,

---

1. See Abram Chayes, "The Role of the Judge in Public Law Litigation," *Harvard Law Review* 89 (1976): 1281–1317; Owen Fiss, *The Civil Rights Injunction* (Bloomington: Indiana University Press, 1978); Donald Horowitz, *The Courts and Social Policy* (Washington, D.C.: Brookings Institution, 1977).

such as the Nuremberg prosecutors' theories of Nazi war planning as a conspiracy and of groups such as the gestapo and SS as "criminal organizations."[2] Such theories have recently been revived in the Czech "lustration" laws declaring the Communist Party of Czechoslovakia from 1948 to 1989 a criminal organization, and presuming the incapacity for public service of persons whose names appeared on secret-police lists of collaborators.[3]

But just as often broad-agency arguments are urged not in pursuit of legal redress in court, but of official or unofficial actions effecting moral redress—compensation of a whole class of persons, or of people with some plausible claim to be their legal descendants, for wrongs done them (or their ancestors) by another class. Such claims are evidently most manageable if they can be made both by and against identifiable persons or legal entities representing them or their successors in interest: for example, the reparations claims against the U.S. government by the Japanese Americans interned during World War II,[4] the claims of native American tribes for restitution of tribal lands,[5] the claims of present-day West Germans for return of property confiscated in the East zone after 1949,[6] the claims of freed slaves after the Civil War for a share of the very plantation lands they had once worked,[7] or even the reparations paid in the 1950s by the West German government (as the legal successor to the Third Reich) to the state of Israel (as the moral

---

2. Telford Taylor, *Anatomy of the Nuremberg Trials* (Boston: Little, Brown, 1992), 501–33, 583–87. For examples of collective or corporate liability in ordinary judicial contexts, both civil and criminal, see Larry May, *The Morality of Groups* (Notre Dame: University of Notre Dame Press, 1987); Joseph Vining, *Legal Identity: The Coming of Age of Public Law* (New Haven: Yale University Press, 1978); Stephen Yeazell, *From Medieval Group Litigation to the Modern Class Action* (New Haven: Yale University Press, 1987).

3. Tina Rosenberg, *The Haunted Land: Facing Europe's Ghosts after Communism* (New York: Random House, 1995).

4. For a comprehensive account of the internees' claims and their legal basis by the lawyer who litigated the claims, see Peter Irons, *Justice at War* (Berkeley: University of California Press, 1993).

5. For a useful recent summary treatment of these claims, see Nell Jessup Newton, "Compensation, Reparations and Restitution: Indian Property Claims in the United States," *Georgia Law Review* 28 (1994): 453–80.

6. The German Unification Treaty distinguishes between expropriations between 1945 and 1949 under Soviet occupation, which are considered irreversible (though, under a 1991 decision of the German Constitutional Court, requiring compensation) and by the German Democratic Republic after 1949, which, subject to overriding legislation to encourage investments, must be restored.

7. See Eric Foner, *Reconstruction: America's Unfinished Revolution, 1863–1877* (New York: Oxford University Press, 1988).

representative of world Jewry).[8] But of course groups making such claims may conceive of victim and perpetrator classes much more generally and loosely—all freedmen and their descendants, for example, against all slaveholders and traders and their descendants, or all blacks (those who have suffered from the legacy of the wrong) against all whites (those who have profited).[9]

Actions taken to undo collective injustices don't always, to be sure, involve compensation or return of property. They may take the form of apologies, or acknowledgment of responsibility for harm, or official ceremonies of remembrance meant to prevent repetition of past errors. The "Truth Commission" that the Chilean government set up after the period of military rule to investigate the abuses of the Pinochet regime took as one of its tasks that of trying to record, as accurately as the files would allow, the fate of every dead or missing person who might have been the victim of the regime and the probable cause of death or disappearance.[10] Or just the opposite: the regime may try to cancel past sins by forgiving and forgetting, granting pardons or general amnesties, or by willing collective oblivion, by maintaining official silence, keeping references to the unjust period out of public discourse and education. The restorers of Chilean democracy—at the military's insistence—followed this path as well, granting a general amnesty for human rights abuses and naming only army or police units, not individual perpetrators, as their causes.

3. Last are what I'll call *structural* approaches: more concerned to attribute injustice to bad structures than bad agents and to attempt to undo the injustices by reforming the structures. The historical enterprise takes the form of a search for explanations rather than a search for villainous agents and attribution of blame; the remedial enterprise is directed to altering institutions, systems, and incentives rather than to exacting punishment or liability. The remedies may include the deliberate erasure of memory, such as when the public monuments and street names of the old regime are obliterated (as in East Berlin twice in modern times, once when the communists took over after the war and now

---

8. Adenauer-Ben Gurion Agreement (1953).

9. Are Marxist-Leninist revolutionary expropriations of the bourgeoisie-as-whole in favor of workers and peasants examples? In their effects, yes, because they penalize one class of agents for another's benefit. In theory of course they are structural.

10. Phillip E. Berryman, trans., *Report of the Chilean National Commission on Truth and Reconciliation* (Notre Dame: University of Notre Dame Press, 1993).

again after they have fallen). That all sounds terribly mild, but naturally it needn't be: notoriously the leading examples of structural approaches to past injustices are Marxist-Leninist regimes, whose structural remedies have led them to expropriate and sometimes physically eliminate whole classes that have stood in the path of the march of history; the victims probably didn't feel any better about it because they were targeted as structures and not agents. Liberal regimes—the subject of the present chapter—also take structural approaches, but they are usually (though by no means always) constrained in their use of more drastic restructurings by liberal norms of legalism and democratic politics.

I started out by saying that each type of response to injustice is embedded in a history; it comes with a story attached of how history went off the track.

The view of history embedded in the corrective justice model is profoundly conservative, in the literal sense of the term. It reduces past or even continuing injustice to the isolated acts of a handful of bad agents: exceptional and abnormal disruptions of a normal law-abiding order. Nothing out of the way has happened except that a few villains or monsters spun out of control and in the process injured a few victims. Ingo Müller's recent work on German jurists after the war furnishes terrible examples of this mentality at its most extreme. The judges asserted their faith in the continuity of an autonomous legal community and doctrinal tradition even through the Third Reich, when the tradition was overlaid—but in the official view only superficially—with a thin layer of alien matter, distinctively Nazi statutes. For these judges, the only real interruption in tradition was that of the dark "tragic" period of occupation, 1945–50. (The faith was sustained on a real continuity in personnel, for denazification efforts hardly touched the judiciary at all.) The courts purged very few statutes as "distinctively National Socialist" and confined the "criminal" agents of the regime to a tiny number of malefactors: Hitler and his immediate circle. Thus when postwar German courts tried even murders committed by lower-level Nazis, they took the view that only Hitler, Himmler, and a few others could be considered "perpetrators" of these crimes; anyone lower down, even if he pulled the trigger, was merely an "accomplice."[11]

Amnesties and pardons seem at first to be insisting on discontinu-

---

11. Ingo Müller, *Hitler's Justice: The Courts of the Third Reich* (Cambridge: Harvard University Press, 1991), 249–60.

ity rather than continuity with the past: it is time to put that unfortunate business behind us, to write a final line—or Schlusstrich, as the Germans say—under it, to make a fresh start. This is especially so when the new regime begins with an amnesty for leading perpetrators of the worst injustices—in some cases because the perpetrators, like the Chilean military, have insisted upon amnesty as a condition of the new regime's establishment; or, in other cases because the new regime, in a spirit of reconciliation, calls a halt to prosecution of perpetrators, as with the German and Allied wave of amnesties, pardons, and statutes of limitation for National Socialist crimes in the late 1940s and the 1950s.[12]

But of course, as these examples suggest, willed oblivion is sometimes the most conservative story of all: it brackets the period of injustice as a historical accident, an outlying event in the general stream, so atypical as not to be worth mentioning, with no origins traceable to the prior period or implications for the present one. The injustice epoch drops out of memory altogether, and history resumes at the point where it left the track.

Treating the old injustices as ordinary crimes or torts, on the other hand, does at least send a signal to the world about historical discontinuity as well as continuity. The criminal trial with elaborate due process safeguards, modeled in Nuremberg, dramatizes the difference between the arbitrary cruelty of the unjust regime and the new regime's regard for truth and fair procedure. Adenauer's agreement to pay 3 billion deutsche marks in reparations to the state of Israel was less an attempt to compensate for the Final Solution, for which no compensation could ever have been enough, than to demonstrate to the Western nations with which Germany sought to integrate that the reconstructed Germany acknowledged its past and accepted responsibility for the predecessor regime's crimes, but was itself a reformed and chastened people, free of the Nazi taint. Still, there is no escaping the implicit conservatism of corrective justice, its implication that all debts are paid; and the period of reparations (Wiedergutmachung) is now generally regarded in Germany in a darker light, as a kind of exorcism by which the government tried to pay for "silence and a good conscience"[13] and to avoid confronting either the Nazi past or its many lingering traces.

---

12. For example, Law on the Granting of Immunity (Dec. 31, 1949; 1 [1949] B.g.b. 37); Law of July 17, 1954 (1 [1954] B.g.b. 203).

13. Saul Friedlander and Corinna Coulmas, "German Leftists come to Grips with the Past," *Holocaust & Genocide Studies* 6 (1991): 33.

In this chapter I want to focus on a particular type of forward-look-ing response to epochal injustice: the restructuring response, the poli-cies directed not at individuals but at institutions, cultures, and social structures, the social engineering strategies designed to rearrange the social system so that its organizations will lack the capacities and in-centives to repeat the injustices. The most radical policies of restructur-ing would seem even more than the policy of deliberate forgetting to re-pudiate the past—or to treat it at best, as in Marxist eschatology, as merely a set of preparatory stages for a revolutionary present that, when actualized, will negate everything that has prepared the way. But just as backward-looking corrections of injustice also point forward to a soci-ety committed to justice in the future, so too do proposals for even rad-ical restructuring rely on narratives of continuity—of traditions and tra-jectories of evolutionary change.

After the American Civil War the most radical proposals—the most radical, that is, aside from emancipation itself, which effected a massive uncompensated transfer of property from slaveholders to freedmen—were the various plans to confiscate large Southern plantations and break them up into forty-acre lots for distribution or sale-by-preemption to the freedmen. The nominal legal basis was corrective—punishment of rebellion and collection of delinquent Federal taxes. A few such lands actually were distributed through tax sales and Sherman's field orders. The most ambitious plan was Thaddeus Stevens's to confiscate 394 mil-lion acres from seventy thousand of the "chief rebels" (about 5 per cent of the South's white families) for distribution to freedmen. Stevens did put forward a compensatory rationale founded in Lockean labor theory: "[The freedmen] have earned this, they have worked upon the land for ages, and they are entitled to it."[14] Just compensation for long services rendered and never paid was apparently also the basis on which most of the freedmen claimed the right to their share of land.[15] But the radi-cals' main motive was to transform the political economy of the South and in consequence its political sociology. The analysis drew upon the central historical narratives of American political experience: the liberal, Scottish Enlightenment and civic-republican histories of the rise of lib-erty through the destruction of "feudal" estates, hierarchies, and

---

14. Thaddeus Stevens, quoted in Kenneth Stampp, *The Era of Reconstruction, 1865–1877* (New York: Knopf, 1965), 122.

15. See Leon Litwack, *Been in the Storm So Long: The Aftermath of Slavery* (New York: Oxford University Press, 1979), 399—408.

"monopolies," and of the foundation of both personal freedom and democratic institutions on decentralized ownership, the economic independence of a self-sufficient "yeoman" middle class of freeholders and small traders. So long as the planter class controlled the land, the freed slaves could never attain enough "independence" to establish a political counterforce.

> Nothing is so likely to make a man a good citizen as to make him a freeholder. Nothing will so multiply the productions of the South as to divide it into small farms. Nothing will make men so industrious and moral as to let them feel that they are above want and are the owners of the soil which they till. . . . No people will ever be republican in spirit and practice where a few own immense manors and the masses are landless. Small independent landholders are the support and guardians of republican liberty.[16]

With the economic basis of the planter class destroyed and the land occupied by yeoman farmers, the South could at last be launched on the evolutionary path to a free society (and not incidentally, ensure the Republican party an unbreakable lock on Congress for some time to come).

A very similar ideology and underlying set of historical assumptions informed an important school of policy-makers defining American structural reform objectives for the occupation and reconstruction of Germany and Japan. There were many conflicting American objectives.[17] Some officials—generally the most conservative, prizing above all the restoration of economic stability and civic order administered through existing elites—adopted a narrow-agency view of Nazism as a criminal "outlaw state" concentrated in a few top officials. Others favored a broader view that fascist and militarist ideologies had infected large numbers in mass and leadership institutions and required a wider purge. Structural approaches to history and reconstruction (setting aside the most drastic and soonest-abandoned structural approach, the

---

16. Thaddeus Stevens, quoted in Eric Foner, *Politics and Ideology in the Age of the Civil War* (Oxford: Oxford University Press, 1980), 135.

17. For useful summaries, see Walter Dorn, "The Debate over American Occupation Policy in Germany in 1944 to 1945," *Political Science Quarterly* 72 (1957): 481–96; Lutz Niethammer, *Entnazifizierung in Bayern* (Frankfurt am Main: Fischer, 1972), 32–68.

Morgenthau Plan for the total destruction of German industrial capacity) seem to have been most common among intellectuals engaged in postwar planning,[18] and these approaches were briefly influential, if far from always dominant, in the first two years of occupation policy. The basic insight was the same as the classical American liberal republican history: that the paradigmatic movement of "progressive" societies was from status to contract, from the "feudalism" of fixed social statuses and of labor tied to land to the free movement of land, labor, and capital; from concentrated land ownership and state-sponsored monopolies to decentralized ownership and competitive enterprise; and that personal freedom and the stability of democratic political institutions in turn in the West, especially in the United States, had rested on the development of a broad property-owning middle class and sufficient social mobility to open access to that class through hard work and talent. By 1945 this history had been brought up to date with a Progressive addendum, in the recognition that the large-scale organizations of industrialized economies had fundamentally changed the political sociology of liberalism: evidently, the ideal of independent proprietorship of a farm of business for nearly everyone had become impossible, and wage-labor or tenant-farmer status the permanent condition of millions. In the conditions of industrial society, democracy had to be sustained on a different basis, and this basis, in Progressive-New Deal thinking, could be generated by public policies encouraging a wide distribution of wealth and access to educational opportunity and combining the breakup of "excessive" concentrations of economic power with the strategic creation of plural and countervailing sources of power, in the trade unions. A new middle class would thus be created out of high-wage labor with job security, craft workers, industrial workers, and white-collar workers within the organizations. Thus the twin dangers would be avoided of a state dominated by industrial plutocrats and of a marginalized and disaffected working class susceptible to communist agitators and fascist dictators. (It was not yet widely appreciated that Hitler had come to

---

18. The intellectuals were concentrated in the Office of Strategic Services: the core was a remarkable group of German émigré scholars: Franz Neumann, Hajo Holborn, Otto Kirchheimer, Felix Gilbert, and Carl-Joachim Friedrich. The bible of this group was Neumann's structural analysis of Nazism in Behemoth: *The Structure and Practice of National Socialism* (Oxford: Oxford University Press, 1942). See Barry Katz, *Foreign Intelligence: Research and Analysis in the Office of Strategic Services, 1942-45* (Cambridge: Harvard University Press, 1989), for an account of this group and its work.

power on the votes of the middle-class, not the working-class, electorate).

This then was what Progressive liberals and social democrats assumed to have been the exemplary history of Western democracies. By the terms of this model Germany and Japan had taken a deviant path to modernity—the thesis that historians now refer to as the "special path," or Sonderweg, thesis. In Germany especially industrialization had not been the project of a middle class committed to liberalism by its opposition to "feudal" landowners and an authoritarian and monopolistic state; it had rather been a "revolution from above," instigated by a thoroughly authoritarian state of officials recruited from hereditary great landowners and officer corps, devoted to traditional hierarchies and privileges, hostile to parliamentary democracy, and prone to expansionist foreign policies. In such a social structure, the state had created giant industrial cartels in its own image and cemented its power by alliance with them, the great landowning interests, and the army, against the threat of social democracy and independent trade unions.

This liberal Progressive view of history significantly influenced U.S. occupation policies in the American zone of Germany. The occupation set about what was probably the most comprehensive program of deliberate social engineering designed to produce the institutions, social structure, and culture of a liberal democratic republic in which Americans had ever engaged, even including the first decades of its own republic-building history and the radical plans for Southern reconstruction. Incidentally the more sophisticated of the reformers, who included a good many German exiles, denied that they were simply trying to remake Germany in the American image: they tried to establish continuities for all their reforms with prior experiments in German democracy, those of 1848 and especially the Weimar Republic. The acknowledged purpose was to break the hold of the old authoritarian elements—through land reform and the breakup of heavy industry, of the press syndicates, and of the elite-schooling monopolies that controlled access to the higher occupations—and to stimulate the formation of plural local from-the-bottom-up organizations: local political parties, regional newspapers, collective bargaining units at the plant level.

The most ambitious because by far the most administratively demanding component of the policy was denazification—which the liberal-progressive planners in the State Department, OSS, and SWNCC saw less as a punitive program than as the crucial prerequisite to positive reconstruction.[19] Key offices in the key institutions had to be staffed with people committed to the values of the new order.

As is well known, both these plans for radical reconstruction—in the post–Civil War South and U.S. zone of Germany—met with predictable fierce resistance and in any case came rapidly into collision with competing policies, serving competing objectives, and attached to competing narratives of continuity, that in short order were to overwhelm them. The two experiences exhibit some remarkable likenesses. Promises under Reconstruction to redistribute plantation lands—to the vast disappointment of the freedmen who had trusted in them—never materialized; the few lands that had been distributed, as in the Sea Islands experiment, were returned to their former white owners. Instead of being yeoman freeholders, the freedmen found themselves once more in subordinate farm labor, initially as contract laborers coerced into Freedmen's Bureau–supervised contracts and tied to the land by vagrancy and enticement statutes, later as debt peons or sharecroppers.[20] Along the way, of course, they were also disenfranchised and resegregated by both law and custom.

For the Southern planters, the Civil War amendments had changed only the formal status of their black labor force; the task now was simply to work around the legal restrictions to reattach black laborers to their former masters and to preserve stratification by caste. Theirs was the narrative of "Redemption"—the reclaiming of "traditional" states' rights, customs, and labor practices after the interruptions of invasion and occupation policies: a recovery of continuity. For the Northern coalition that backed off the promise of Reconstruction to build a foundation for republican liberty by providing the freedmen with homesteads, the main strategy for linking the redeemed South to the liberal narratives of American history was through a much narrower construction of the end point of Western development as the possession of a formally equal chance at achieving, whatever the individual's starting point, self-sufficiency through free labor. Any additional attempts to distribute advantages to the freedmen would be a *reactionary* step backwards into a preliberal regime of dependence-inducing "paternalism" and race-based

---

19. See John H. Herz, "The Fiasco of Denazification in Germany," *Political Science Quarterly* 63 (1948): 569–94; and Herz, "Denazification and Related Policies", in *From Dictatorship to Democracy*, ed. John H. Herz (Westport, Conn.: Greenwood Press, 1982), 15–38.

20. See Willie Lee Rose, *Rehearsal for Reconstruction* (Indianapolis: Bobbs-Merrill, 1964); Foner, *Politics and Ideology*.

preferences and disabilities.[21] In the minds of Northern whites, the abolitionist view of the South as a pocket of feudal backwardness gave way to a "culture of conciliation" in which Northern whites combined deliberate forgetting—amnesty and amnesia for the rebellion and the "sins" of slavery—with adoption of Southern whites' own romantic myths of Redemption as recovery of a chivalric and aristocratic past, the continuing of a tradition in which blacks knew, and gratefully accepted, their servile place.[22]

The results of Allied occupation "democratization" policies in Germany were more mixed—and still very much disputed among historians: they pushed through the adoption of the Basic Law; they did stimulate political party formation and competition, especially at the Land level; and they are generally credited with helping to create an independent press. The policies aimed at breaking the hold of traditional "authoritarian" elites and broadening the bases of social opportunity had very limited success. Radical decartelization and deconcentration policies were discarded by 1947 as obstacles to the more important goals of restoring German industrial capacity and integration with Western trade; though a milder form of decartelization directed at coal and iron was revived in 1950.[23] The U.S. preference for factory-level collective bargaining over bread-and-butter issues and its hostility to German efforts to construct institutions for corporatist bargaining (codetermination, workers' councils, centralized national unions) seem to have had the immediate effect of suppressing new grassroots initiatives for the governance of industry and thus of maintaining the hold of the old elites.[24] The educational reforms—directed at replacing the old system of class-based tracking and at modernizing the curriculum, especially

21. Gerald Jaynes, *Branches Without Roots* (Oxford: Oxford University Press, 1986), 16–23; Foner, *Reconstruction*, 237; Aviam Soifer, "The Paradox of Paternalism and Laissez-Faire Constitutionalism," *Law & History Review* 5 (1987): 249–79.

22. Nina Silber, *The Romance of Reunion: Northerners and the South, 1865–1900* (Chapel Hill: University of North Carolina Press, 1993), 108–9.

23. Volker Berghahn, *The Americanization of West German Industry, 1945–73* (Cambridge: Cambridge University Press, 1986), 84–110. See also Albert Diegmann, "American Deconcentration Policy in the Ruhr Coal Industry," in *American Policy and the Reconstruction of West Germany, 1945–55*, ed. Jeffry M. Diefendorf et al. (Cambridge: Cambridge University Press, 1993), 197–215.

24. Diethelm Prowe, "German Democratization as Conservative Restabilization: The Impact of American Policy," in *American Policy and the Reconstruction of West Germany, 1945–55*, ed. Jeffry M. Diefendorf et al. (Cambridge: Cambridge University Press, 1993), 307–29.

in social sciences, languages, and history—aroused formidable conservative resistance and succeeded only in establishing the Free University in West Berlin and a handful of integrated comprehensive schools in a few Länder.[25] Only the officer corps was genuinely reconstructed, thanks in large part to the Soviet zone's destruction of its economic base in the Junker estates.

Denazification was a notoriously expensive fiasco. The most resented of all Allied occupation policies—opposition to denazification was the only issue that united all postwar German parties—it was also the most ineffectual. Administrative mass processing by inexperienced personnel inflicted fines and dismissals on thousands of small fry, while the larger fish were spared because they were urgently needed for rebuilding efforts, or were better equipped to take advantage of backlogs to delay their cases, or had emigrated from the East where no Westerner could know what they had done. Soon after the process was turned over to reluctant German tribunals to complete, it became largely a "follower-factory (Mitläuferfabrik)" process for reclassifying serious "offenders." By the time the U.S. Congress called a lurching halt to the process in 1948, sacrificing it to the more pressing need for reliable and unresentful allies against communism, the very meaning of the term *denazification* had changed from a process for the purging of Nazis from positions of influence to a process for rehabilitating former Nazis to declare them eligible to return to their positions of influence.[26] The policies paid the penalty for overambition and confusion of aims. The liberal democratizers in the American zone had the largely structural aim, as in Japan, of replacing wholesale the top echelons of the German ruling class, and to this end drew up an appendix of high offices in bureaucracy, military, and industry [Control Council Directive #24]; but the Germans never accepted this appendix—and invariably characterized denazification in strictly agency-based terms as devoted to finding

---

25. James Tent, *Mission on the Rhine: Reeducation and Denazification in American-Occupied Germany* (Chicago: University of Chicago Press, 1983); Jutta-B. Lange-Quassowski, *Neuordnung oder Restauration? Das Demokratiekonzept der amerikanischen Besatzungsmacht und die politische Sozialisation der Westdeutschen* (Opladen: Leske, 1979); Lange-Quassowki, "Coming to Terms with the Nazi Past: Schools, Media, and the Formation of Opinion", in *From Dictatorship to Democracy*, ed. John Herz (Westport, Conn.: Greenwood Press, 1982), 83–103.

26. John Gimbel, *A German Community under American Occupation* (Stanford: Stanford University Press, 1961); John D. Montgomery, *Forced to be Free* (Chicago: University of Chicago Press, 1957); Niethammer, *Entnazifizierung*.

and punishing the worst Nazis. No matter how often the Allies characterized the tribunals as merely administrative, negative findings did after all carry penalties such as fines, confiscation, and deprivation of office with legal tenure. To the extent the proceedings were purportedly narrow-agency-based, targeting the worst offenders, they were visibly unjust, since the categories and presumptions on the questionnaires were necessarily crude, the administrative process necessarily summary, and the role of grudge informers in accusing and of good personal and clerical connections in exonerating so pervasive. To the extent they were based on broad-agency notions of collective liability, they were especially resented by a people already inclined, in the ruins of war, mass dislocation, and occupation, to see themselves collectively not as victimizers but as victims.

As structural remedies, at the same time, the denazification policies were vastly over- and underinclusive: by requiring all Germans older than eighteen to be screened instead of targeting high functionaries, they simply never got around to reviewing major institutions like the civil service; and by conflating the authoritarian elements they wished to purge with Nazi party membership, they passed over entirely traditional elites who had never joined the party but had done its bidding, had helped to undermine Weimar, and now sought to restore the institutions of the Kaiserreich. More decisively, the structural objectives of the purges conflicted fundamentally with other structural aims. As Volker Berghahn concisely put it:

> A de-Nazification policy which would have taken to task those individuals who made a major contribution to sustaining the Hitler regime would have touched the social and economic power structures of the Western zones much more radically than the Allies were prepared to permit. Neither the kind of economic system nor the society they were trying to reconstruct could exist without the expertise of the administrative, managerial and technical elites which had collaborated with Hitler.[27]

Resistance to the social reforms of the democratizers, and the shift of Allied policy focus from "reform" to stabilization with the division of

---

27. Volker Berghahn, *Modern Germany*, 2d ed., (Cambridge: Cambridge University Press, 1987), 187.

Germany and the onset of the cold war, naturally drew upon alternative narratives of Germany history and the placing of that history within the wider history of the West. The history of Germany as dangerous so long as it remained an authoritarian departure from the Western modernizing norm was temporarily shelved in favor of another much closer to the orthodox German view. In this view the mistakes not to be repeated were, first, those of Versailles, in which overly punitive peace terms had pushed the resentful German electorate into the grasp of a dictator who promised to restore national pride; second, the descent into economic chaos that had turned the stabilizing element of the middle class politically volatile; and finally, the weakness of the state, the inability of the fragile republic to defend itself against antidemocratic subversion—which in postwar conditions, under the prevailing analysis equating fascism and communism as variant forms of a single pathology of "totalitarianism," was subversion from the Left. American policy thus turned away from internal reform of German social structure to a strategy of integrating Germany with the Western Allies—with industry through the Schuman Plan, with trade through the Marshall Plan, with defense through rearmament under NATO command—and of subsidizing the economic miracle. This policy actually drew upon a much older narrative of Atlantic culture, the *doux commerce* thesis of Montesquieu and the Scottish Enlightenment, to the effect that turning to commercial pursuits is the best dissolver of a nation's warlike spirit. And in the meantime, the structural-reform ambitions of the democratizing liberals, especially decartelization and denazification, were discredited by being compared to the drastic and ruthless social restructurings that had been carried out on the other side of the Iron Curtain.

Some among the German elites, at the same time, were able to rescue from the failures and turnabouts of Allied policy an identity based on rather different, often very conservative, ideas of continuity. For some conservatives membership in NATO reaffirmed Germany's historical geopolitical and cultural identity as the buffer Middle European state defending the humanistic values of the West from the barbarian hordes of the East. Traditional elites took care to affirm the positive value of Germany's deviant path (minus Hitler's regrettable excesses, which in this period were dealt with by silence): we like our Sonderweg, they said, we have no wish to be like America. The churches, which Americans in one of the most ludicrous cultural mistranslations had assumed to be "progressive" forces for democracy because of their dislike of Nazism, had most of all disliked Nazism for its ideology of progress and its populist policies: they undertook to retain the elite schooling tracks such as the Gymnasium and to ensure their devotion to Germany's ancient humanist past and "Christian values," most especially by requiring Latin and Greek. As of 1950, former Nazi party members were still in, or returned to, high positions in the civil service, judiciary, universities, and industry. Ingo Müller has described the official ideology as one of continuity of legal and civil-service traditions, the only interruption in continuity being denazification itself. Some "victims" of denazification received compensation in the civil courts; most important, a statute was passed (May 11, 1951) under the authority of Article 131 of the Basic Law, giving all those civil servants dismissed since 1945 a legal right to reinstatement and back pay. "For all practical purposes," as Müller comments acidly, "former membership in the Nazi party became a requirement for joining the civil service."[28] Yet though the most unregenerate of the elites, such as the judges and law professors, insisted on continuity, probably the most widespread strategy toward the Third Reich in the 1950s was deliberate oblivion. General amnesties were passed for Nazi crimes; the Allies pardoned or commuted sentences for most of the war criminals; the teaching of history in the schools and universities ended with Bismarck. Until the subject was sharply revived in the youth revolts of the 1960s, the Nazi period was treated as an inexplicable outbreak of exceptional criminality, and a general silence on the period descended.[29]

This has so far been an attempt to outline some general approaches that liberal societies have adopted to undoing historical injustice and the kinds of narratives of continuity and reformation that are attached to each approach, and also to begin to fill in the outline with some examples. Now I want to turn to the most enduring legacy of historical injustice in the United States, the subordination of its black people, and to ask how the conflicts over U.S. legal policy in the Second Reconstruction, especially affirmative action policies, fit into the general scheme I've outlined. These debates yield a rich if bewildering variety of positions.

---

28. Müller, *Nazi Justice*, 205.
29. Richard Evans, *In Hitler's Shadow* (New York: Pantheon, 1989), 11–12; Ian Buruma, *The Wages of Guilt: Memories of War in Germany and Japan* (New York: Farrar, Straus & Giroux, 1994), 56.

Agency-based models, to recall the basics of the scheme, are those that frame the injustice as a harm committed by perpetrators upon victims, the undoing of which requires a make-whole remedy commensurate with the wrong. The result aims simply to remove blemishes that dot a landscape of historical normality.

Narrow agency is now the position commonly identified with legal conservatives, such as those who staffed the Office of Legal Counsel and the Civil Rights Division of the Justice Department in the Reagan administration as well as the "right" wing of the U.S. Supreme Court, Justices Antonin Scalia and Clarence Thomas. The essence of the position is simple: slavery and Jim Crow were great historical injustices because they violated the historically established American basic norm of formally equal legal treatment of persons, or color blindness. These injustices were undone and the principle vindicated in the Reconstruction Amendments, *Brown v. Board of Education,* and the Civil Rights Act of 1964. Thus: (1) any state action (or private action subject to the antidiscrimination statutes) that directs preferential treatment of any racial group, including "affirmative action" intended to benefit historically disadvantaged groups, is unlawful as violating the color blindness principle prohibiting any use of racial categories as the basis of legal action; (2) the only persisting injustice that is legally cognizable is that of provable individual acts of racial animus directed against specific persons; and (3) whites who are disadvantaged by race-conscious policies are themselves victims of discrimination who must be legally made whole.[30] We are not to look back at older sins that may have contributed to present racial inequalities; and we are certainly not to contrive broad structural approaches to remedying them that benefit the victims of history: that is not justice, but "social engineering."[31]

The position seems at first glance completely antihistorical: After the Civil Rights Act of 1964, America is born anew and born into a presumptive condition of color blindness; the past has become simply irrelevant, except as its traces linger in the animus that occasionally flares into an isolated act of discrimination. Like much else in Reagan's ideology, the position owes something to the old myth of the American

---

30. The position has been advanced on innumerable occasions—perhaps in its purest and most powerful form in the Brief of the Solicitor General filed in Wygant v. Jackson Board of Education, 476 U.S. 267 (1986).

31. Morris Abram, "Fair Shakers and Social Engineers," *Harvard Law Review* 99 (1986): 1312–26.

Adam, who upon arriving in America sheds the Old World's burdens of history and original sin and becomes free to reinvent himself. If the myth is an awkward fit to the situation of peoples descended from forcibly imported slaves, it can be made to fit by imagining 1964 as the date of their "arrival": once released from legal disabilities, blacks have since been free to compete on equal terms.

Yet inspected more closely, the position, like narrow-agency positions generally, is rooted in a conservative historical narrative of deep continuities subjected to temporary interruptions and deviations. The major civil rights tracts of President Reagan's lawyers and other conservative theorists of race relations consist in large part of elaborate historical justifications.[32] The main use of these histories is to establish that America's traditional, indeed Constitutional, Grundnorm of legal equality means color blindness and nothing else. Calling for authority on dead radicals, conservatives claim as precursors not only the authors of the Declaration of Independence, Lincoln, and the elder Justice Harlan, but also the abolitionists, Frederick Douglass, and the leaders of the early civil rights movement—Thurgood Marshall and the NAACP, Martin Luther King and the SCLC, and Hubert Humphrey and the other sponsors of the 1964 Civil Rights Act. If the deep continuity is in America's commitment to color blindness, any departure from it is a momentary deviation or anomaly. Indeed, in this view the original Constitution itself was an anomaly, a regrettable compromise with principle, unfortunately necessary at the time to bring the Southern states into the Federal Union. Slavery and state-mandated segregation were anomalies too.

On a par with those evils, and equally representing departure from historically established principle, is the general trend of federal civil rights policy after 1965—judicial remedies in the form of "affirmative and comprehensive" school-integration plans intended to remedy not simply present discrete discriminatory acts but also the effects of historical discrimination: the adoption of statistical disparate-impact measures of employment discrimination and the imposition of novel requirements of federal contractors and grantees of numerical "quotas, goals, and timetables" measuring affirmative action favoring specific groups. The great discontinuity, as pictured in these conservative histo-

---

32. For representative conservative histories of race relations, see Terry Eastland and William J. Bennett, *Counting by Race: Equality from the Founding Fathers to Bakke and Weber* (New York: Basic Books, 1979); Clink Bolick, *Changing Course* (New Brunswick, NJ: Transaction Books, 1988).

ries, is thus between American liberalism's "traditional" pursuit of color-blind equal treatment and the modern civil rights coalition's mania for quotas and proportional representation. "To pursue the concept of racial entitlement—even for the most admirable and benign of purposes—is to reinforce and preserve for future mischief the way of thinking that produced race slavery, race privilege, and race hatred."[33]

All histories select, but the omissions of this one are breathtaking. The most obvious problem with the narrative is its attempt to find firm ground in history for a basic norm to which, until quite recently, few whites ever subscribed. For most of our history it was generally assumed even in the free Northern states that blacks were, like women, a taken-for-granted exception to the norm of liberal equality; and indeed, especially in the South, that the confining of blacks to menial labor, either slave or free, was a necessary condition to the equal liberty and full citizenship of the white population. The norm of "color blindness" in the conservative narratives is at best a deeply buried immanent norm, a norm in long gestation, carried before its full realization only by a handful of mavericks, marginals, and outsiders: abolitionists, Radical Republicans, a lone dissenting Supreme Court justice (Harlan), and the moderate wing of the modern civil rights movements. In order to represent color blindness as the modern consensus norm, the conservative histories must leave out—and they do leave out—all the modern history that would help explain why liberal centrists after 1964 turned to affirmative action strategies. They represent the period from the 1954 *Brown* case as an irenic period of steady progress in race relations, in which one legal barrier after another fell to full legal citizenship and in which the irrationality of racism evaporated in the sunlight of modernity, rather than one of ferocious and continuing white resistance—including resistance by many people in the current conservative leadership, which that same leadership has exploited to its considerable political advantage.[34]

---

33. Adarand Constructors, Inc. v. Pena, 63 U.S.L.W. 4523 (1995) (Scalia, J., concurring).

34. See generally Thomas Byrne Edsall and Mary D. Edsall, *Chain Reaction: The Impact of Race, Rights and Taxes on American Politics* (New York: Norton, 1992). As Randall Kennedy has grimly pointed out, the record of opposition of conservative leaders like Ronald Reagan to virtually all past civil rights legislation and enforcement tends to make people who believe in civil rights more than a little skeptical of present conservatives' claims to good faith on racial justice issues; Randall Kennedy, "Persuasion and Distrust: A Comment on the Affirmative Action Debate," *Harvard Law Review* 99 (1986): 1327–46. Nathan Glazer, in *Affirmative Discrimination* (New York: Basic Books, 1975) is one of the few neoconservative writers who deals at all candidly with the fact of white resistance.

The other major omission is any mention of the ways other than simple official color blindness in which civil rights movements and their supporters have defined justice for themselves. If names like King's are to be invoked as authority for the content of norms of justice, some notice should be taken of what the moderate civil rights activists actually believed: that the opposite of "segregation" was "integration," which has many possible meanings but clearly meant something more than the formally color-blind state of "desegregation," freedom from government race-based classifications. The injustice of segregation was not so much that the government made formal distinctions between races but that those distinctions served to enforce white supremacy, a caste system based on race, a system of pervasive economic, social, and cultural subordination. It was the evident failure of the purely formal and negative definition of justice as "color blindness" to make much headway against the institutions and customs of the caste system—practices that continued effectively to shut most blacks out of access to the jobs, schools, and neighborhoods that are the mobility channels of American society—which prompted the 1965 turn in civil rights policies.

Those post-1965 policies are very complex; but there's a mainstream or centrist set of justifications for them that is best described as *broad*-agency based. Their defenders agree with the narrow-agency view that the overall goal of civil rights policy is the remedy of past acts of discrimination but favor a much expanded method and scope of showing violations and obtaining relief, an approach that favors collective liability and group-based remedies. Broad-agency histories lay emphasis on the bitter experience with enforcement after *Brown*, which demonstrated that white resistance to integration was so fierce, tactics to evade court orders or fake compliance with hiring directives under cover of race-neutral devices so ingenious, as to make case-by-case proof of intent wholly ineffectual. The policy emphasis therefore shifted to wholesale enforcement, the substitution of statistical "effect" for individual "intent" as prima facie proof of discrimination, and measurable, monitorable, quantitative measures of relief in order to circumvent evasion and make enforcement burdens manageable. All these remedies could have been, and were, justified as an interim means to the ultimate end of color-blind equal treatment: "To get beyond race, we must first take account of race." (Eventually, of course, affirmative action policies developed their own vested interests and constituencies, some of whom began to rationalize the policies in very different terms: as programs designed to foster proportional representation to minorities in certain job categories and institutions—either as compensation for past injustice or to meet the independent structural goal of "diversity.") As both judicial and executive branches were broadening both remedies and the classes entitled to them, the courts rapidly expanded the class of perpetrators well beyond present violators to those in the deep past—the officials who, even if long ago, had committed the fateful acts of intentional segregation that resulted in today's barriers to equal access.

Kathleen Sullivan has pointed out how the emphasis of the courts on "sins" of past discrimination, the framing of affirmative action claims as corrective responses to undo, repair, or compensate for past discrimination, helps maintain the perpetrator-victim (agency-based) focus of the public debate on affirmative action.[35] Whites say, We had nothing personally to do with the enslavement and oppression of blacks: indeed, our ancestors were being slaughtered by cossacks or starved out of Ireland at the time; it is now we who are victimized by departures from equal treatment and strict legality. Blacks respond in a similar discourse of agency, but broaden the frame: We are the descendants of those who were collectively victimized and we demand reparations; and we are still currently victimized by the continuing traces of historical wrongs and continued practice of the institutions and criteria of "merit" that were created in order to suppress us; and we demand access to the places we would have occupied but for this legacy. The earliest proposals for affirmative action, in fact, seem to have originated from civil rights leaders using this broad compensatory rationale. James Farmer of CORE, in testimony before the House Judiciary Committee in 1963, resolutely denied favoring either "quotas" or the displacement of white workers, but he did argue that in choosing between a white and black candidate of roughly equal qualifications, an employer should choose the black candidate. Rep. Rodino asked, "Isn't this preferential?"

> FARMER: Well, you could call it preferential, you could call it compensatory, but sir, we have been seeking . . .
> RODINO: Isn't that discriminating against a white who may have been innocent of any discrimination against anyone else in that time?

---

35. Kathleen Sullivan, "Sins of Discrimination", *Harvard Law Review* 100 (1986): 78–98.

FARMER: You see, none of us are really innocent because we are caught in a society, the social system which has tolerated segregation. Negroes have received special treatment all their lives. They have received special treatment for 350 years. All we are asking for, all I am asking for now is some special treatment to overcome the effects of the long special treatment of a negative sort we have had in the past.[36]

If one conceives of the problem in such broad-agency terms, the make-whole remedy calls for a massive counterfactual thought experiment: imagine what positions in society and the economy living blacks would have attained had they not been subject to acts of racist injustice. The presumptive answer, the late Ronald Fiscus argued, is that they would have been represented in all places in the class and occupational structure in proportion to their numbers in the population.[37] (The conservative objection to the counterfactual, that this assumption makes no allowances for generic differences in culture affecting economically valuable talents, abilities, and preferences is well taken; but so too is the response that, but for racism, those differences might not have developed.) The argument is a perfectly sensible one within the "bad actor" framework of legalism—one undoes the bad acts by undoing their effects, with the effects assessed by reference to where history would have brought the victimized group without the acts. But the assessment it calls for can only be performed very abstractly. The history of the United States, its entire economy, society, politics, and racial and ethnic composition, would have been so different without slavery that one couldn't even begin to guess what American society would look like now.

The argument from history then, has supported broad-agency claims to compensation or make-whole remedies for past injuries—in the form of grants of immediate access to positions of advantage. The response of some conservatives to this kind of argument is a sort of historical fatalism—history is a long unbroken recital of brutality and in-

---

36. Quoted in Hugh Davis Graham, *The Civil Rights Era: Origins and Development of National Policy, 1960–1972* (Oxford: Oxford University Press, 1990), 109.

37. Ronald Jerry Fiscus, *The Constitutional Logic of Affirmative Action* (Durham, N.C.: Duke University Press, 1992). For a recent extension of the argument, see Cheryl Harris, "Whiteness as Property," *Harvard Law Review* 106 (1993): 1709–91.

justice, of ancient wrongs that cannot possibly be set right.[38] The legal system cannot possibly correct all these wrongs; all it can do is try to maintain the conditions for equal justice in the present and police current violations. But the usual conservative response relies on a much more optimistic set of assertions—that if the conditions of equal justice are satisfied, they actually operate so as to erase historical (and every other sort of unmerited) inequities in very short order. The equal treatment required by color blindness is coextensive with the conditions of "equal opportunity" to be evaluated according to merit, talent, ability, character. The problem, this very familiar argument goes, with post-1965 civil rights policy is that it replaced the goal of "equality of opportunity" with that of "equality of results," that is, proportional representation of minorities in all situations of advantage.

The argument is built on an important structural premise with its own supporting history: that American society has gradually but finally evolved to the stage where, now that formal race distinctions have been removed, and residual acts of discrimination motivated by animus are legally forbidden, existing opportunity structures will in fact distribute rewards according to merit and talent. (Note: not according to "marginal product"—this is a moral argument, made in the moral language of classical liberalism, not a neoclassical economic argument.) The conditions of equal opportunity do not need to be created; they have arrived. Sometimes the assertion rests explicitly on a historical foundation, such as Thomas Sowell's thesis that the moment formal barriers were removed, blacks occupied the same relation to opportunity as any other immigrant groups. If then some blacks have not succeeded, we should not presume discrimination—many groups have faced that and succeeded, including West Indian blacks—but rather inherent deficiencies in African-American culture.

But of course the argument is much older than Sowell: it is the Jack-

---

38. In some recent decisions, courts have been giving as a reason for refusing to recognize Indian land claims the long, sorry, brutal history of white depredations of Indian lands; as if the repeated trampling of justice in the past could in itself be a justification for denying it now. Some judges are inclined to spread the blame: whites brutalized Indians, Indians brutalized whites, it all evens out. See Aviam Soifer, "Objects in Mirror are Closer Than They Appear," *Georgia Law Review* 28 (1994): 533–53; and Joseph Singer, "Well Settled? The Increasing Weight of History in American Indian Land Claims," *Georgia Law Review* 28 (1994): 481–532, for caustic and insightful reflections on this use of history in Indian lands cases.

sonian, or Free Soil, or simply classical liberal argument that welds liberal legalism to liberal political and moral economy: that in a society structured so that all have formally equal rights, and none have special disabilities or special privileges (in the form of "class legislation" of which the most important type is monopoly privileges), all will be free to compete on equal terms and to rise to the level befitting their efforts, virtues, and talents. In such a society history ceases to count; for we all are free to make our own destiny. It was exactly this argument that Northern conservatives used, after the Civil War, to defeat special legislation and protective measures on behalf the black freedmen—that they were "paternalist" measures, obnoxious both as conferring special advantages on blacks and not on whites and as promoting in their beneficiaries habits of dependence rather than sturdy self-reliance.[39] Its genius lies in its equation of existing legal baseline entitlements with the condition of natural justice, any departures from which require extraordinary justification. What might be otherwise a controversial—and potentially very productive—structural argument about what the social preconditions of genuinely equal opportunity really might be is presented as a taken-for-granted premise, that the status quo baseline is required by the rule of law.[40]

The use of history in this argument, then, is to show that by long-

---

39. See Soifer, "Paradox of Paternalism"; Eric Schnapper, "Affirmative Action and the Legislative History of the Fourteenth Amendment," *Virginia Law Review* 71 (1985): 753–98.

40. For a typical, though valuable because unusually explicit, conflation of simple legality with equal opportunity (current race-neutral rules distribute opportunity equally; thus any redistribution would offend the rule of law) see Abram, "Fair Shakers and Social Engineers." The irony is that Abram is an old New Dealer, who would probably not object to structural alteration of the baselines to redistribute opportunity more equally, so long as the policy did not employ explicit racial criteria.

Of course, many conservatives do use structural and pragmatic arguments against affirmative action as well. In a bad mood, conservatives accuse rights activists of simply "rent seeking," securing places for themselves by law that they couldn't earn, creating jobs (or getting votes by creating jobs) for themselves in quota-monitoring bureaucracies. More generously they allow that the policies are "well-intentioned" but have inefficient and perverse effects—the proliferation of offensive racial and ethnic categories in public life (Jim Crow redivivus) and unseemly intergroup competition for benefits accruing to victim status; damage to merit selection on the basis of individual worth; intrusive bureaucratic and judicial meddling in the decisions of employers and public authorities to run their shops as they see fit; adverse effects on quality, productivity, and competence of work; stigmatization of genuinely competent minorities. Yet the argument at the end usually returns to the perpetrator-victim perspective: affirmative action isn't simply bad policy, it's injustice to whites.

standing historical tradition—from which slavery and legalized segregation were unfortunate deviations[41]—the history of a group's situation
is irrelevant to its legal status; those who would make it relevant again
are repeating the errors of the racist past.[42] The legal history supporting
the argument is that the formal-equality color-blind norm is the norm
established by our traditions. The social history supporting the structural argument is that where the norm prevails, historical disadvantage
can be overcome because opportunity structures have in fact operated
to give everyone a fair shake.

Both the legalist and the structural positions have been challenged,
from Right, Left, and Center. Each challenge uses history both to derive
a different baseline norm and to assert that historical experience has either strayed from or never lived up to that norm.

The libertarian Right position is a purified version of the Center-
Right thesis that has dominated conservative policy. The Center-Right
thesis, recall, holds that by 1964 the American polity had actually
achieved the conditions of an equal treatment, equal opportunity society. It had finally fulfilled the norm from which post-1965 policy was to
deviate. The more radical, or libertarian Right, position is that the norm
came closest to fulfillment at the high point of classical-legal liberalism

---

41. The modern conservative view of the history of racial subordination is one curiously detached from collective membership in the American polity: racial subordination
never had much to do with people like us, and anyway it all happened a long time ago.
In this aspect, American conservatism somewhat resembles the self-distancing of German
conservatives from the Nazis as vulgar barbarians. In his reply to Justice Marshall's bi-
centennial speech charging that the Federal Constitution was "defective from the start"
because of its entrenchment of slavery, William Bradford Reynolds argued that the Founding Fathers were regretfully forced to compromise with slavery in order to induce the
southern states to join the Union; but that they really provided for its eventual extinction
by enacting a structure of government designed to promote evolving liberties, and an
amendment process in Article 5, whereby the fruits of that evolution could be, in time,
constitutionally encoded. (See Reynolds, "Another View: Our Magnificent Constitution,"
Vanderbilt Law Review 40 (1987): 1343–51. One might complain that this account rather too
rapidly skates over the fact that the constitutional structure itself was intended to insure
the southern states against the risk that the northern ones would someday confiscate their
property by emancipation. Similarly, libertarian critics fault the "state," conceived as an
alien excrescence, for the rules that have restricted black opportunity, almost as if the state
and its rules were independent of society, as if Alabama government in the 1920s, for instance, were an entity wholly distinct from the white planter class.

42. The rich irony of this posture is that for many years the moderate conservative
position on civil rights was a wholly Burkean one, that the accumulated weight of American traditions and customs of racial segregation lay so heavy on society that change must
perforce be very slow; anyone who demanded equality now, even of the most formal kind,
was an abstract radical with no historical sense!

in the late nineteenth and early twentieth century, the era of *Lochner v. New York*. Where it has been distorted is in the long history of government policies that exceed the proper constitutional limits of the police power: among these policies—in addition to regulation of wages, hours, and work conditions; occupational licensing and entry barriers to trades; legislation allowing union closed shops and other exercises of monopoly power—are laws enforcing segregation. The legal-historical argument is devoted to establishing not the current distribution of entitlements and institutions, but the laissez-faire regime as the baseline constitution of a liberal society.[43] Unfortunately, in this view, the ideal baseline conditions have been so disfigured by extensions of the police power that broad structural remedies will be needed to restore it—widespread repeal of regulatory laws, of the Wagner Act, of the public-school monopoly's claim to taxes, of the minimum wage, and of the anti-discrimination laws themselves.

This structural argument is a largely abstract one from political economy, albeit with some empirical-historical support. The basic argument is that cartels of whites to exclude blacks from opportunity are inherently unstable because competitive pressures make it rational to hire (recruit, educate) qualified blacks; that such discrimination as remains despite those pressures is likely to be only residual and in any case justified as an exercise of individual autonomy (an eccentric preference for racism over profits); and finally that any attempt to remedy residual discrimination through law will be, like virtually all forms of regulation, captured by special ("rent-seeking") interests and over-extended as well as inefficiently intrusive into rational market calculations of employers. The history that backs this up is a general catalog of regulatory failures informed by Chicago public-choice and regulatory economics' very dim view of state capacity and proneness to capture; a much thinner—and highly contested—history supporting the point about the instability of racial cartels, and some economic studies purporting to show that industrialization and competition, not the civil rights laws, were the driving force behind black employment gains in the 1960s and 1970s.

The liberal-centrist argument dominated mainstream civil rights enforcement policy since 1965. It argues from a traditional legal baseline

---

43. See Richard Epstein, *Forbidden Grounds: The Case against Employment Discrimination Laws* (Cambridge: Harvard University Press, 1992); Clint Bolick, *Unfinished Business* (San Francisco: Pacific Research Institute, 1990).

not of classical but of Progressive-New Deal liberalism that the government has to aggressively restructure some markets and institutions in order to equalize conditions of opportunity. The long history of discrimination has left a continuing legacy of disadvantage—racial stereotypes, educational deficits, isolation in environments spatially removed from jobs and prone to the self-destructiveness of despair. In the famous words of President Johnson's Howard University speech: "You do not take a person who for years has been hobbled by chains and liberate him, bring him up to the starting point of a race, and then say, 'You are free to compete with all the others,' and still justly believe you have been completely fair. . . . We seek not just freedom, but opportunity—not just legal equity but human ability—not just equality as a right and a theory but equality as a fact and as a result."[44] In context, this is a perfectly centrist statement—not an argument for a legislated equality of everything (whatever that might mean) but for promoting the concrete conditions of an equality of opportunity, a race from an equalized starting point. The justification for affirmative action contained in it is partly agency-based—compensation in the form of preferences for handicaps or, as with veterans' preferences, for wounds incurred in consequence of one's country's policies—but is also structural: our job is to demolish these historically created barriers. In the structural view, affirmative action is simply one among many plans, as Kathleen Sullivan has put it, in "the architecture of a racially integrated future."[45] It was designed to help bypass traditional barriers to black advancement, like father-son sponsorship recruitment to craft unions, or political patronage or family network access to contracts and jobs, or tests or formal credentials bearing no provable relationship to job performance; it was designed to increase the size of the black middle class as rapidly as possible—by expanding the number of jobs in the public sector and encouraging recruitment to colleges and professional schools—partly to produce more professionals and businesses to serve black populations, but largely to help overcome racial stereotypes derived from the evident social fact that society whitens out toward the top, blackens out toward the bottom. Part of the historical argument backing this approach is that racism and social-economic exclusion and isolation have fed on each other; so conversely do integration and equal opportunity: "Green follows

44. Public Papers of the Presidents: Johnson, 1965, I, 636.
45. Sullivan, "Sins of Discrimination," 80.

white"—resources go where the whites are; living in white communities and attending white schools have powerful neighborhood effects. The general notion is that the *ultimate end point* to be achieved is equal opportunity, meritocracy, and market rationality; but that progress toward this goal has had to be jump-started against cultural resistance (historically embedded racism, conscious, unconscious, and "statistical") and across structural barriers of isolation.

All the positions just described share the common structural goal of the equal opportunity society, although their divergences make abundantly clear how vague and elastic that goal is. Right-centrists, the current conservative majority in Congress and the Supreme Court, believe the conditions of equal opportunity have already been achieved, disfigured only by affirmative action preferences. Left-centrists, the dominant civil rights coalition until recently, believe in policies designed to construct those conditions against the lingering traces of racism. Libertarians believe that only radical restructuring of the legal framework can effectively restore the laissez-faire conditions of the equal opportunity society.

Two other important traditions of thought and action regarding racial equality are in near-total eclipse at present but worth mentioning both for their prominence in the past of the struggle for racial equality and the critical insight they offer to the present.

One might be called a Left–social democratic view. This view uses a yet different baseline norm, an image of equality that also has deep roots in the American past: the antisubordination norm of American Revolutionary radicalism, artisanal republicanism, radical Reconstruction, the industrial labor movements, and, in the civil rights movement, the ideas of King and his chief theorist, Bayard Rustin. In this view the main obstacles to fulfillment of the norm of equality-as-antisubordination is the segmented economy—beginning with slavery itself, conceived of as a labor system structured by class as well as race distinctions, and continuing after emancipation as race is used by white capitalists to maintain the dual economy by dividing white laborers against black ones. At its peak of political influence in the Johnson administration, the civil rights coalition came close to persuading the federal government to undertake the massive full employment programs that would be needed to help overcome dualism; but it ran out of money and political support and had to settle for the War on Poverty program instead, in effect a very modest program combining a few jobs for black community activists with an expansion of traditional relief for the poor. Nixon's affirmative action programs, such as in public contract set-asides (the Philadelphia Plan), were a similar form of tokenism, an attempt to co-opt and buy out the most politically articulate blacks and gain some protection against urban protest, while not antagonizing the southern whites and northern white-ethnics who were his main political base.[46]

Another once-important vision of race-neutral equality has today—tragically—almost disappeared altogether: integration. A serious integrationist strategy would take the historically established baseline norm (of *Brown* and the 1960s civil rights movements) to be "color blindness" in the sense of a social state in which racial distinctions would simply cease to have much practical significance in the distribution of access to valuable social goods, opportunities, and respect. The achievement of such a state would actually require a social transformation of vast dimensions—one in which racial differences were not actually *perceived* as relevant. This would probably have to be an integrated, intermarried society in which pigmentation was distributed randomly across occupations, neighborhoods, and classes. For as long as one race persistently and disproportionately ends up at the bottom of the social ladder, with the highest crime and unemployment rates or, if employed, the crummiest, dead-end minimum wage jobs with no benefits and no advancement, society can't possibly be "color blind"; everyone will notice this distribution and will draw strong conclusions from it—either about the capacities of members of the group or the injustice of race-based inequality. It is at least as plausible that policies on the model of the forced-integration model of the military, compelling different racial groups to associate, work together, and get to know each other, is likely to promote judgments on the content of one's character rather than the color of one's skin. Arguably something like this theory was historically tested in integration of the military, of the work forces of large public and private employers, in housing, and in education through school busing. Busing is now widely, but probably incorrectly[47] perceived as

---

46. H. R. Haldeman's recently published *Diaries* (New York: G. P. Putnam's Sons, 1994) suggest a considerably more cynical set of motives: that Nixon continued and intensified executive affirmative action policies because he well knew how divisive they were and hoped to reap the political benefits of backlash from their implementation.

47. See Jennifer Hochschild, *The New American Dilemma* (New Haven: Yale University Press, 1984) for evidence suggesting the successes of compelled school integration where it was seriously tried and supported by local authorities.

having been a complete failure, inducing massive "white flight" and disaffection with civil rights. Yet in the military, the perception is exactly the opposite, that forced integration has both worked and been accepted as legitimate.

Many in the civil rights movement have, however, become disillusioned with the ideal of race-neutral equality of opportunity altogether. They oppose to it a culturally pluralist norm of proportional representation, developed from a political model of social goods that also has a long history backing it up. The argument here is that the economy and society are and always have been riddled with special deals and preferences—that opportunity is distributed more by patronage and old-boys' networks, often based on ethnicity, than by "merit" (and indeed that what is called "merit" often has a large unspoken ethnic component); and thus what equal opportunity should mean as a practical matter is equal access to patronage. The demand for proportional representation is simply the demand to be included in the Great American Pork Barrel: We'll give up our claims to special treatment when you give up your ethnic political patronage, sponsorship of relatives for police and firefighter jobs, admission of legacies to colleges, tax preferences, veterans preferences, farm price supports, and the like. The supporting history argues that optimists like Sowell are mistaken in their basic proposition that outsider groups can advance only by adapting their cultures to produce skills in current demand by markets, for social advancement has in fact accrued to newcomer groups who were able to forge coalitions to obtain political power. When those groups have included blacks, blacks have advanced; when, as has happened much more frequently, blacks have been squeezed out of power, they have suffered. Affirmative action from this perspective is sometimes quite a conservative policy: it asks only for parity in patronage, slotting of minorities into established structures of jobs and access to jobs, rather than a restructuring of the labor market or a flattening of class divisions. There is, however, a more radical version that argues that what is valued as "meritorious" or skills is itself a product of cultural-racial categories; valued skills are just the skills that people on top happen to have, and what needs changing is what is valued—a redistribution of rewards based on a redistribution of recognition of value to plural cultural traits.

The civil rights experience has also given rise to some profoundly pessimistic views of history as an unbroken chronicle of hopes raised only to be dashed, promises made only to be broken, gains won only to be eroded, a grim testimony to the permanence of racism.[48] The dominant baseline norm in these narratives is white supremacy, a historical constant disturbed only by the occasional and ephemeral achievements of black struggle and resistance. The *Brown* case and the civil rights policies that followed it may look progressive but often serve only as covers for newer and subtler forms of racism: integrationism conveys the message that blacks living or educated apart from whites are necessarily inferior; equal opportunity norms privilege the forms of "merit" possessed by whites and thus serve to legitimate a racially skewed distribution of jobs and social goods; "color blindness" itself is simply a stratagem of subordination. The more optimistic believers in the permanence of racism hold out hope for separatist strategies of cultural preservation and economic development, sometimes coupled with broad-agency claims for financing by means of reparations or other concessions from white society. The more pessimistic often end up, ironically, in the same dark cul-de-sac as conservative historical fatalism—skepticism toward all claims of progress either achievable or already achieved, resignation to the inevitability of oppression in one or another of its endlessly mutable forms.

The examples have been intended to illustrate the kinds of policies and remedies to which those who would confront past injustices may be led by commitment to narrow-agency, broad-agency, or structural approaches. May one conclude anything from the examples about the relative value of the approaches? Nothing simple, anyway; certainly nothing like a clear recommendation for one approach over the others for general adoption.

I do, however, emerge from this exercise with strengthened, though not unqualified, respect for the structural modes of responding to great injustices and a sharper awareness of the deficiencies of the agency-based ones of either the broad or narrow kind—with a qualified preference, that is, for both structural explanations and structural (or social-engineering) remedies over correction of wrongs or redemption of sin. Or, to express this in another way that less rigidly distinguishes law from morality and morality from politics: a society's most valuable response to historical injustice may often be to assume collective moral re-

---

48. See, for example, Harold Cruse, *Plural But Equal* (New York: William Morrow, 1987); Derrick Bell, *And We Are Not Saved* (New York: Basic Books, 1987).

sponsibility for structural understanding and, where this is possible, structural reform.

The recent legal controversies over affirmative action are particularly good illustrations. There is a productive and substantive political debate about what structural barriers still impede the equal participation of blacks in American society and how those barriers may be removed. A small, but only small, fraction of that debate would worry about the wisdom or folly, the costs and benefits, of affirmative action—whether, as conservatives suggest, it helps mostly middle-class blacks and stigmatizes even them; whether, as liberals insist, it has not only helped create a substantial black middle and professional class but also significantly improved black working-class opportunities with no discernible adverse effects on productivity; whether, as some social democrats such as William Julius Wilson and Theda Skocpol suggest, race-targeted social programs have reached the limits of likely effectiveness and in view of their great political unpopularity should be replaced by class-based policies targeted to the poor. These are all issues well worth trying to resolve. But in general political rhetoric they have been swamped by a controversy, as unilluminating as it is politically explosive, about whether blacks are innocent victims or authors of their own misfortunes and whether whites are guilty perpetrators or themselves innocent victims of racist acts. For this is how the U.S. Supreme Court has chosen to frame the issue, setting limits supposedly derived from constitutional law on how policy-makers, private institutions, and employers may go about trying to remedy the problem of continuing de facto American apartheid. As Sullivan puts it, "If casting affirmative action as compensation invites protests about windfalls to nonvictims, casting it as punishment invites protests about unfairness to nonsinners. Viewed through the lens of retributive justice, a focus on sin begets claims of innocence."[49] The hunt for narrow agency then rapidly expands into broad, into general group blaming, and competing claims to the status of innocent victim. For blacks the morality of their claim is so obvious—all those generations of uncompensated slave labor; exploited sharecropper labor; exclusion from jobs, housing, and education; lynchings, false arrests, and unequal treatment by white courts and juries; and insult and humiliation have built up an enormous social debt. If, having been shoved to the back of the line for most of our history, they now

49. Sullivan, "Sins of Discrimination," 94.

ask for a place at the front, that is to ask for simple justice. But the agency model says, to displace anyone from the line, it is not sufficient that you be victims; they also have to be perpetrators. As Kyle Haselden put it more than twenty years ago: "It leaves with the descendants of the exploiters a guilt they cannot cancel and with the descendants of the exploited a debt they cannot collect."[50] Groups personalized as the eternal oppressor, who are asked to feel permanently guilty, turn instead angry and defensive, especially if they too belong to the struggling and victimized groups of history; while groups whose identity is constituted through the history of victimization and cannot claim material benefits except through their status of victim must fight to retain that status and to compete for it against other victimized groups. In such a system for allocating moral claims, to lose the status of innocent victim—which one begins to do the moment one achieves any place or power in society— is to risk losing not only preference but part of one's identity.[51]

Agency-based theories are really of very limited use as a framework either for understanding systemic or societywide injustice or for ensuring it does not happen again. To take account of systemic injustice, the framework has sometimes to be expanded past the breaking point of plausibility—to make institutions and collective social movements into "defendants" by stretching notions of "conspiracy" and inventing new ones, such the Nuremberg prosecutors' theory of "organizational liability" for the SS and gestapo; or, as in broad-agency theories, by the use of concepts such as "collective guilt" or "institutional racism," which confusingly deny agency at the instant of affirming it because they suggest that guilt inheres simply in being present in the historical situation, or in being descended from those who were, and is thus inescapable. The legalist notion of wrongs as departures from baseline norms, deviations from acceptable patterns of conduct, is an awkward conceptual fit to a regime that, with the support or complicity of most of civil society, is organized around the wholesale commission of wrongful acts. I don't mean, I hasten to say, that killing Jews or enslaving blacks by the millions is not wrong, that such acts can escape moral condemnation by virtue of having been approved by nation-states and engaged in by thousands of perpetrators. But if you see Nazism or slav-

---

50. Quoted in Graham, *Civil Rights Era*, 113.

51. For a particularly acute critique of group identity construction through history of victimization, see Guyora Binder, "Representing Nazism: Advocacy and Identity at the Trial of Klaus Barbie," *Yale Law Journal* 98 (1989): 1321–83.

ery or segregation primarily as "violations" of some standard of natural or international law or "human rights," you are not making progress toward understanding them as social systems that made sense to and were accepted by many people at the time as authority relations, or labor systems, or caste systems, or bureaucratic routines, or simply regrettable necessities.[52] In the aftermath of the *Brown* decision, for instance, most lawyers entrapped in the legalist paradigm seemed to find it painfully difficult to explain what exactly *was* wrong with enforced apartheid, separate-but-[formally]-equal racial segregation. The Supreme Court itself came up with the rather odd theory that the wrong was infliction of psychological harm, but it gave no account of the context that would explain why the harm could not be avoided, as the old *Plessy* case had airily suggested, by simply having the black race put a different psychological construction on separation—a "multicultural" construction, for instance, to the effect that each racial "culture" was best preserved as a matter of policy by development in separate enclaves. The theory that compelled segregation violates the neutral "color blindness" norm by making racial status legally relevant does no better, for race distinctions are only obnoxious within a social structure that visits them with obnoxious consequences. In this strange legalist desert, it is a profound relief to come across Charles Black's celebrated article on "The Lawfulness of the Segregation Decisions,"[53] which pointed out what everyone already knew but could not say—partly because uncertain of its legal relevance, partly because unwilling to indict an entire region's habitual "way of life"—that segregation was one among many devices used to enforce a system of racial subordination, to keep blacks literally "in their place" in a hierarchy of orders.

Besides obscuring structural understanding, an emphasis on legal

---

52. In Germany, as Geoff Eley has pointed out, "concentrating opprobrium in the Nazi's crimes against the Jews" has served a right-wing agenda by obscuring Nazism's "relationship to a larger constellation of right-wing interests and belief. Once the problem of Nazism has been circumscribed in this way, questions of deeper origins and Germany's broader responsibility—that is, the more difficult and disturbing questions of Nazism's structural rootedness in German society at large—are easier to keep from the agenda." Eley, "Nazism, Politics and the Image of the Past," *Past and Present* 121 (November 1988): 174. Whether the Holocaust itself, as opposed to the other routine social-systemic practices of National Socialism, will always resist historical understanding, even of the structural kind, is a open question. See Dan Diner, ed., *Ist der NS Geschichte?* (Frankfurt am Main: Fischer, 1987).

53. Charles Black, "The Lawfulness of the Segregation Decisions," *Yale Law Journal* 69 (1960): 421–30.

or moral redress can also inhibit structural solutions that may, in the end, accomplish much more. An obvious present-day example is the vogue for restitution of property to precommunist owners in Eastern Europe. Restitution is problematic enough on grounds of justice and fairness: why (as Jon Elster has asked) should it be those who have suffered this particular form of material loss, as compared to those denied the opportunity to contract or deprived of their privacy, dignity, liberty, and expressive freedom, who have first call on compensation?[54] More pragmatically, where restitution rights have been legislated, as in the former East Germany, they have sufficiently clouded titles so as to significantly inhibit investment (and as a result have been since largely overridden by subsequent statutes).[55] Some of the same difficulties, and even greater ones as well, surround the current revivals of interest (probably given fresh encouragement by the movements to reclaim Indian lands and compensate the Japanese-American internees) in reparations for American blacks, for their ancestors' forced transit, enslavement, and subsequent continuing legal subordination. Skepticism about reparations proposals commonly, and reasonably, tends to focus on issues of practical administrability, the problems of classification posed by trying to identify, at this remove, the current "victims of slavery," not to mention the beneficiaries of slavery who must be taxed to compensate them.[56] But the major objections seem to me structural. Group liability theories of such enormous breadth have to rely on such attenuated notions of blame and causation as to subvert their moral plausibility and thus undermine possibilities of political fraternity, creating resentment even between those who might be coalition partners in a politics that cast them as allies instead of historical villains. Groups who have suffered more immediate wrongs—including perhaps wrongs in which U.S. policies were complicit, such as torture or killing of their families by Salvadoran death squads—might wonder why *they* are being taxed to remedy such historically distant evils. Even more to the

---

54. Jon Elster, "On Doing What One Can," *East European Constitutional Review* 1 (summer 1992): 15–17.

55. Hans-Werner and Gerlinde Sinn, *Jumpstart* (Cambridge: MIT Press, 1993); Ulrich Preuss, "Restitution vs. Investment," *East European Constitutional Review* 1 (summer 1992): 22–24.

56. The administrability problem is addressed at length and with great ingenuity in Boris Bittker, *The Case for Black Reparations* New York: Random House, 1973); and the classification problem in Mari Matsuda, "Looking from the Bottom: Critical Legal Studies and Reparations," *Harvard Civil Rights-Civil Liberties Law Review* 22 (1987), 323–99.

point: What would a one-time payment of compensation to the current generation accomplish? Wouldn't the money, if we could raise the political will for it, be better spent on institutional investment such as job training, drug treatment, scholarships, income credits for the working poor, public works, and other measures to address structural unemployment? Reparations payments, even when designed primarily as apology and symbolic atonement rather than literal compensation, are best given to the living victims of injustices that are firmly in the past; indeed, one of the messages intended by reparations is that the wrong is over and done with. When the wrong is continuing, the result of historically entrenched structural conditions, the last message the regime should be encouraged to send is that the current generation's obligations vis-à-vis the wrong can be satisfied with damages.

The familiar critique of structural explanations and of structural approaches to remedies is that they obscure the moral significance of social injustice: if the system is at fault, no one is at fault; if everything is structure, there is no agency; tout comprendre, c'est tout pardonner; the moral differences disappear between planning and following, between gross brutality and indifference, between fanatic enthusiasm and grudging complicity, between murder and guard duty, between profiteering and indirect benefit (getting the position that otherwise would have been occupied by the black or Jew or bourgeois), between those who enthusiastically supported and profited from the system, those who quietly but unhappily went along, those who performed small acts of kindness in the leeways of the system, and those who actively resisted. Most observers of President Reagan's peculiar speech at Bitburg Cemetery, which placed the Waffen-SS troops buried there on a moral equivalence with all the other "victims" of the Nazi regime, felt its terrible inappropriateness.[57] Without acknowledgment of wrongful, personal agency, there is no shame; without shame, no assumption of responsibility, no possibility of redemption. (It is frequently said of the official German response to the Third Reich even to this day—that although there is increasing identification with the regime's victims, there is still little sense of implication in the death machinery of many "ordi-

<hr/>

57. For reflections on the moral meanings of the Bitburg ceremony, see Geoffrey Hartman, ed., *Bitburg in Moral and Political Perspective* (Bloomington: Indiana University Press, 1986). Reagan's speech of course was anything but structural; it relied on the "outlaw" theory of Nazism as the work of a criminal gang, with neither roots in previous history nor continuities into the present, which had victimized all Germans.

nary" Germans and almost no disposition to identify with active resistors as the true patriots trying to save Germany from itself.) If law describes injustice as abnormality and deviation, structural-historical explanation seems to do just the opposite. Although it may, as we've seen, describe the injustices as the product of a system that itself deviates from some macrohistorical norm or ideal, it nonetheless "normalizes" the unjust acts within the system as its banal and everyday practices.[58]

All true enough; yet in practice it has been the agency-based approaches, rather than the structural ones, that have tended to be exculpatory: the new regime turns on the bad agents as scapegoats for wrongs that derived from the routine functioning of an entire social system. The trials of the worst offenders, the purges of the system's satraps and beneficiaries, even the reparations payments made to the most conspicuous victims, sometimes serve as ritual acts of exorcism of the monstrous, abnormal elements of a system with which, at the time, almost everybody in one way or another went along.[59] (Sometimes, alas, the purges serve no higher purpose than a personal settling of scores or pursuit of political advantage.) One thinks here of the ways in which the French people savagely punished "collaborators" after World War II or of the mass purges of Communist party functionaries that some of the new regimes are undertaking in Eastern Europe for the crimes committed by those regimes. Indeed, some observers have suggested that the quite efficient current West German purges of the former East German bureaucracy, legal system, and universities of political unreliables is intended in part to make up for the earlier failures of both the Weimar and denazification-era regimes to protect themselves against the enemies of democracy; others remark caustically that neither Weimar nor the Fed-

58. This was surely the most commonly made critique of Hannah Arendt's *Eichmann in Jerusalem.*
59. Interestingly enough, in Eastern Europe it has often been the public figures (such as Adam Michnik and Vaclav Havel) with some of the best moral credentials as resistors to former communist regimes who now denounce "lustration" (purging of former communists and informers)—partly because that process would have to rely on the corrupt old regime's secret files to identify offenders, because the mass purge was an instrument of Communist party rule and "we are not like them," and because purging would be a "distraction" from the important business of rebuilding society, but also because in the old regime "everyone" was in some sense implicated: as Havel has put it, "we are all—though naturally to differing extent—responsible for the operation of the totalitarian machinery; none of us is just its victims; we are also its co-creators" (quoted in Maria Łos, "Lustration and Truth-Claims," forthcoming, an exceptionally penetrating analysis of the discourse of purges in East Europe).

eral Republic ever found it difficult to protect themselves against threats from the Left. The proposal of reparations payments to black Americans for the injustices of slavery has drawn support from, among other sources, neoconservatives who see a one-time payment as a way of getting quit of all future African-American claims on their republic's moral sense or purse strings.[60] The late Alan Freeman argued that American race relations policy in the Second Reconstruction adopted the perpetrator-victim model of racial wrongs as harmful deviations from the norms of equal treatment and meritocracy precisely so as to deflect attention from the contribution made by those very norms to maintaining a dual economy.[61] The condemnation of slavery as a departure from liberal norms obscures the extent to which, understood structurally and in context, slavery was indeed a departure from liberal norms and equality but also a precondition to their realization for most of the white population.[62]

Anyway, the moral distinctions are hardly irrelevant to structural responses: even if the new regime is primarily looking to structural reform rather than the punishment of individuals, if there is a choice in the matter it may not want to maintain in power those agents who in past times were the chief bearers of the old regime, carriers of its genes, as it were, agents who have developed attachments to its values and careers and vested interests around reproducing its habits and manipulative and duplicitous modes of operation, and who reflexively oppose anyone who would reform it. Even if most of them were just opportunists rather than true believers, do you want your own Rechtstaat staffed with opportunists?[63]

---

60. Charles Krauthammer, "Reparations for Black Americans," *Time* 136 (31 December 1990): 18.

61. Alan Freeman, "Legitimating Racial Discrimination Through Antidiscrimination Law," *Minnesota Law Review* 62 (1978): 1049–1119.

62. Edmund S. Morgan, *American Slavery: American Freedom* (New York: Norton, 1975).

63. Moral and structural concerns in this area may, however, irreconcilably conflict. From a moral point of view the ideological idealist who saw himself as selflessly building a classless utopia may be a considerably more attractive figure than the cynical apparatchik who joined the party for careerist privileges. (Admittedly by the time of the collapse of 1989 there were probably very few genuine idealists left.) The idealist, however, has no useful role in the new regime; like the many tenured professors of Marxism-Leninism in the universities, he will be out of a job, whereas the cynical apparatchik may make quite a competent capitalist manager.

Is it fair, people ask, that those who had comfortable office jobs under the Communists should still have them today, when ordinary people are having to tighten their belts? Is it fair that members of the *nomenklatura* are exploiting the uncertain legal conditions of privatization to take over as capitalists the enterprises they had previously commanded as Communists?[64]

This example, however, does highlight one of the central problems with structural approaches: since they work upon institutions and groups (as broad-agency approaches do too), they involve wholesale treatment of the peoples in those groups without reference to particular deserts and thus treat them to some extent inevitably as objects. From the point of view of the people hurt, the impersonality of the reform process, its indifference to their displacement and loss, is the most frightening thing about it. Whether or not the reformers legalize or moralize their aims, their victims will surely do so and accuse the new regime of behaving just like the old one, treating people as disposable because of their race, class, or institutional position. Members of liberal societies will, it seems, accept a considerable amount of such dislocation—loss of job, housing, neighborhood—if the structure that imposes it is an impersonal market; much less if it's seen as deliberate policy: they won't treat an affirmative action plan that costs them their job the way they would a plant closing. The Soviet occupiers of the East zone found it easy to denazify, since their structural policies were wholly unconstrained by legalist scruples; they did not feel it necessary to make fine distinctions between Nazis and the bourgeoisie generally or to be cautiously underinclusive in their internment, confiscation, and expulsion policies; and once the new structure was in place, they did not hesitate to declare an abrupt end to denazification and to reemploy in high party positions recanting Nazis who could be useful to them. The Allies, necessarily hampered by legalist concerns about due process, and at the same time far too ambitious in their structural goal of trying to replace wholesale the entire party apparatus while in fact having to make wholesale exceptions in order to staff the recovery, got the worst of both worlds: a mass administrative process that was too cautious and slow to be effective yet still created new martyrs and victims.

64. Timothy Garton Ash, "Eastern Europe: Après le Déluge, Nous," *New York Review of Books* (16 August 1990), 51.

Neither is the relative impersonality of structural explanations of past injustice—historical explanations rather than legal or moral blame fixing—necessarily any less politically controversial than attribution to specific wrongdoers or groups. In the German Historikerstreit, the great "historians' controversy" of 1986-87, the sides were divided by their attachments to diverging structural approaches to explaining Nazism and the Holocaust: some conservatives (to simplify greatly a greatly complex debate) assimilating these events into a generalized twentieth-century crisis of modernity and pattern of mass horrors also exemplified by Stalin's and Pol Pot's massacres; liberals (and leftists) condemning that as a distraction from structural causes in Germany's own authoritarian (and capitalist) past.[65] Instead of focusing attention on needed reforms, history can become a massive subsidiary political battleground on which every monument, every date and proper name for hundreds of years past, is charged with polarized meanings.

There is also no guarantee that structural understandings will not undermine any reform impulse. It so happens that the structural views of history I have mostly been discussing are Whiggish views that see the "normal" past as pointing toward progress, so that the past correctly understood will indicate both the possibility and the directions of reform. One can rescue a similar optimism from critical views of history that assume structures are never determining, that there are always alternative paths to be chosen, that the contingent strategies of agents, especially collectively mobilized political agents, can make a difference at crucial junctures. But structural explanations could just as easily lead to fatalism, despair, and paralysis: we are in the grip of processes (the decline of the West, the globalization of the capitalist world system) in which domestic-political initiatives are pathetic scratchings on the surface of things. Coulmas and Friedlander have written movingly about the way many German youths, especially of the Left, feel not only overburdened but "mutilated": "the idea that German history is so overwhelming that it [has] crushed its offspring's personality, the free will and the freedom of the individual."[66]

Thus it may be that, quite paradoxically, the reformist possibilities of structural understanding may be restricted to societies whose own traditions make plausible a view of history in which good agents can tri-

---

65. On the Historikerstreit; see Charles Maier, *The Unmasterable Past* (Cambridge: Harvard University Press, 1988); Evans, *In Hitler's Shadow*.

66. Friedlander and Coulmas, "German Leftists come to Grips with the Past," 6.

umph over bad structures. (The West German experience is now very appealing to some liberal reformers in Eastern Europe as an example of how a society with an authoritarian past can be discontinuously remade into a democratic one.) We are lucky enough to be beneficiaries of such traditions, yet in dealing with our racial heritage and dual economy we don't take advantage of our good fortune. Here is a puzzle: why is it that when conservatives excoriate social engineering schemes, the attempts at the "architecture of a racially integrated future," that they find a sympathetic ear? Why must structural claims to be politically acceptable adopt the vocabulary of legalism? After all, structural politics is hardly foreign to our history: America itself is a social engineering scheme, an experiment in liberal-republican society in which many legal policies untried almost anywhere else in world history—inheritance reform, wide distribution of public lands in homesteads, abolition of indentured servitude and imprisonment for debt, married women's property acts, the vast redistribution of property effected in uncompensated emancipation of slaves—have been carried out for the specific purpose of producing the social preconditions of a liberal polity—enhancing political stability, economic prosperity, and civil peace by creating a large middle class and reducing the distance between rich and poor. When we propose social changes for other societies, such as the former communist countries, we seem not to hesitate to recommend, or require as the condition of financial help and political support, very extensive restructurings of social and economic institutions—quite often, alas, in complete disregard of local traditions, continuities, and political consequences. But in our own society we seem to have reached a point of near paralysis in social experiments, less out of complacency than exhaustion.

Justice for All? Marriage and Deprivation of Citizenship in the United States

Nancy F. Cott

In 1924 Mary K., an American-born woman descended from seventeenth-century English colonists, married a man who was, she and he both believed, also an American citizen. He was Taraknath Das, a native of India, a Hindu who had received a certificate of naturalization from a U.S. court in 1914 after eight years of American residence. Shortly after the marriage, however, Mr. Das's naturalization was declared to be illegal and void, and Mary K. Das was also stripped of her citizenship. When she applied for a passport she was refused, on the ground that she had lost her citizenship by her marriage to a man who was an alien ineligible for citizenship.[1]

Just about the same time, another woman arrived in Seattle, Washington—the state where she had been born—expecting to take up her privileges as an American citizen after having spent most of her life in China, where she had married a Chinese man and then been widowed. She was the daughter of Chinese parents; her name was Ng Fung Sing. At Seattle, she was refused admission to the country of her birth. A fed-

---

1. Mary K. Das, "A Woman Without a Country," *Nation* 123, no. 3187 (4 August 1926): 105–6; Emma Wold, "A Woman Bereft of Country," *Equal Rights*, 15 August 1925. Both Mary and Taraknath Das were consequently stateless: while American authorities claimed that Hindus who were deprived of their American citizenship reverted to their former status as British subjects, British law stipulated that any subject who had voluntarily been naturalized in another country lost British nationality. Candice Dawn Bredbenner, "Toward Independent Citizenship: Married Women's Nationality Rights in the United States, 1855–1937" (Ph.D. diss., University of Virginia, 1990), 289–91, first alerted me to this case.

eral court confirmed the immigration officials' judgment that she was a Chinese subject, ineligible for American citizenship and inadmissible to the country.[2]

These incidents—and they are not isolated incidents—occurred because of a conjunction of federal laws declaring married women's status and laws restricting naturalization privileges. I want to look at these series of laws and their meanings here, with several aims in mind. First of all, I am interested in marriage as a public institution, particularly in its relation to the nation-state. What we call marriage, and may commonly think of as an arrangement of private life, is a legal status—one that local, state, and federal governments in the United States have established and that does not itself exist without the state. Marriage has been a means of social ordering, an instrument that keeps in place the social order sanctioned by public authority. In the United States the marriage institution has been a powerful instrument of gender ordering and of racial ordering (so-called antimiscegenation laws, which I will not deal with here, being the most blatant evidence of the latter). At the level of the nation-state, marriage, along with naturalization and immigration policies, is the institution that guards the qualities and characteristics of the "body politic" by controlling sexual reproduction that is deemed legitimate. Marital status and citizenship have been linked together in the United States historically in complex ways, not always the same ways for men and for women, for the alien and the citizen, or for different racial and ethnic groups.

Second, on the assumption that the government of the United States is meant to "establish justice," as the preamble to the Constitution declares, I am interested in how far the laws linking marriage and citizenship can be said to constitute or be compatible with justice. I take as a point of departure Susan Moller Okin's important and effective critical insistence that the history of theorizing about justice—from ancient to contemporary—has by and large assumed that family relations are outside or prior to the realm of social relations where the criteria of justice matter. This assumption not only divides the world into realms of public (where considerations of justice apply) and private (where justice appears irrelevant) but also means, in effect, that the individual to

---

2. Ex parte Fung Sing, 6 F.2d 670 (1925); Waldo Emerson Waltz, *The Nationality of Married Women: A Study of Domestic Policies and International Legislation*, Illinois Studies in the Social Sciences, vol. 22, no. 1 (Urbana: University of Illinois Press, 1937), 46, first alerted me to this case.

whom justice pertains—who is to be subject of and to justice—is not every or any individual, but the one who is a male head of household. To my mind, Okin has argued successfully that this assumption (implicit or explicit) will rob a theory of "justice for all" of its validity. To purport to offer a plan for justice while ignoring male domination and privilege in the family is futile, she contends, because it allows the nurture of the next generation to take place inside an unjust institution.[3]

In stressing the mutually constitutive relation of marriage and the state, I hope to illuminate, in line with Okin's critique, the partiality or falsity of any claim that marriage as an organization of "private" life is exempt from criteria of justice. As I hope my narrative of the impact of marriage on citizenship will make clear, the state is actively involved in creating social and civic relations for both men and women through legal marriages (therefore actively involved in forming and sustaining gender itself). State policies have been central in mandating relations of domination and dependence in the marriage institution in the past and reproducing these for the future through the socialization of future citizens. If a central purpose of governing is to "establish justice," such formative state policies cannot be exempt from criteria of justice. I don't mean to suggest, however, that criteria of justice, especially as enacted into law, are absolute or fixed. There has been tremendous change in public judgment, and also in judicial opinion of what *is* just, over time. Even though changes in the law move not consistently but only fitfully toward enhanced conceptions or enactments of justice (as the history I will relate suggests), nonetheless I think that we have to recognize the social construction of both justice and law and even to applaud that mutability.

Following Robert Gordon, I would argue for the "fundamentally constitutive character of legal relations in social life." In Gordon's simile, "the specific legal practices of a culture are simply dialects of a parent social speech and . . . studying the speech helps you understand the dialect and vice versa."[4] Yet since justice and law are not congruent and

---

3. Susan Moller Okin, *Justice, Gender, and the Family* (New York: Basic Books, 1989). See also Okin's earlier work, *Women in Western Political Thought* (Princeton: Princeton University Press, 1979).

4. "Even a legal system clotted with arcane technicalities is unlikely to depart drastically from the common stock of understanding in the surrounding culture in the methods it uses to categorize social realities, the arguments about facts and values that it recognizes as relevant and persuasive, and the justifications it gives for its exercises of power." Robert Gordon, "Critical Legal Histories," *Stanford Law Review* 57 (1984): 104, 90.

coterminous, and both are socially constructed, the sometime gap, or lag, between them begs for address. Can and do laws only (belatedly) adopt notions of justice that are already vented in social life and general public debate? Or can and do laws create and implement—indeed, invent—new notions of justice? With the alternative posed this starkly, most of us would probably answer, "some of both." I do not mean to determine but simply to raise the issue here, because it seems especially germane to considerations about marriage as an institution linked to citizenship. As long ago as 1847, in the flush of American pretensions to lead the world in democracy, the renowned jurist Justice Joseph Story wrote, "In respect to the powers and rights of married women, the law is by no means abreast of the spirit of the age. Here are seen the old fossil foot-prints of Feudalism. The law relating to women tends to make every family a barony or a monarchy, or a despotism, of which the husband is the baron, king or a despot, and the wife the dependent, serf or slave. . . . Public opinion is a check to legal rules on this subject."[5] Story's view here seems curiously appropriate to the narrative I am going to relate, although the public opinion that formed a "check" was not contemporaneous but subsequent to the legal rules.

The spine of my narrative is provided by congressional actions taken in 1855, 1907, and 1922, which significantly revised the relation between women's marital status and their nationality.[6] Congress also enacted additional modifications in the early 1930s, essentially restoring the relation between marriage and citizenship for women to what it had been before 1855 (ironically enough). An examination of these policy changes and their consequences illuminates the reliance of men's and women's civic statuses on their family positions and, when immigration restriction is brought into the discussion (as it should be), also reveals intersections between civic gender prescriptions and the ethnic and racial formation of the national community.

---

5. J. Story, *Treatise on the Law of Contracts Not under Seal*, 2d ed. (Boston, 1847), quoted in Carol Weisbrod and Pamela Sheingorn, "Reynolds v. United States: Nineteenth-Century Forms of Marriage and the Status of Women," *Connecticut Law Review* 10 (summer 1978): 835.

6. Bredbenner, "Toward Independent Citizenship," is a thorough investigation of the history of married women's nationality rights in Congress and the courts, more concerned with the interaction between that history and immigration law than is Waltz, *Nationality of Married Women*, the preexisting definitive history. I was first interested in this topic by Virginia Sapiro's very compelling article, "Women, Citizenship and Nationality: Immigration and Naturalization Policies in the United States," *Politics and Society* 13, no. 1 (1984): 1–26.

For three-quarters of a century after the American Revolution, women's nationality rights appeared to be about the same as men's. Adhering to the British common-law tradition that nationality was indelible, American law did not assume that a woman's citizenship changed if she married a man of a different citizenship (although the settled presumption of the law was that a woman's domicile, or legal residence, followed that of her husband). A U.S. Supreme Court decision of 1830, *Shanks v. Dupont,* enshrined this doctrine. In it, Justice Story wrote that "marriage with an alien ... produces no dissolution of the native allegiance of the wife. It may change her civil rights, but it does not effect [*sic*] her political rights or privileges."[7]

In 1855, however, the U.S. Congress passed a statute declaring that foreign-born women who married American men became American citizens by marriage.[8] Two aspects of this provision are notable. One is its gender specificity. It gave a particular privilege to American male citizens, to endow their wives with American citizenship. It did not give a parallel privilege to American female citizens—quite the opposite. No American woman got to endow her foreign husband with her nationality. The statute underlined male headship of the marital couple (and therefore of the family and household) as a political norm as well as a social norm. That was even more emphatically so because the same statute affirmed that children born abroad to American fathers—not American mothers—were American citizens. (A bill had earlier been proposed to affirm citizenship for children born abroad to American mothers *or* fathers, but that bill did not succeed.[9])

In its privileging of the male individual as *the* American citizen, this 1855 act brought forward the always-implicit connection between an individual's marital status and his or her civil status. As feminist political theorists from Susan Okin to Carole Pateman have pointed out, the Western contractual political tradition gave great (if implicit) importance to a man's headship of a family—his responsibility for dependent wife and children—as a qualification for him to be a participating mem-

7. Shanks v. Dupont, 3 Pet. 242 (1830), at 246; Waltz, *Nationality of Married Women,* 18–23. See James H. Kettner, *The Development of American Citizenship, 1608–1870* (Chapel Hill: University of North Carolina Press, 1978), on the differences between British and American notions of citizenship in the early republic.

8. *Congressional Globe,* 33d Cong., 1st sess., 13 January 1854, 169–71; *Congressional Globe,* 33d Cong., 2d sess., 20–21 December 1854, 8 February 1855, 91–92, 116, 632, 651.

9. Frank George Franklin, *The Legislative History of Naturalization in the United States from the Revolution to 1861* (Chicago: University of Chicago Press, 1906), 271–74.

ber of the polity.[10] In the minds of the founders of the American republic, marriage, property holding, and heading a family were together
linked to political participation. Discussing political rights in 1776, for
instance, Thomas Jefferson wrote to a friend that he favored "extending
the right of suffrage (or in other words the rights of a citizen) to all who
had a permanent intention of living in the country. Take what circumstances you please as evidence of this, either the having resided a certain time, or having a family, or having property, any or all of them."[11]
In republican theory, the citizen's independence (independence of
means and of judgment) was key; and men's independence was
strongly associated with being married—with the succession to (inher-
ited) property or livelihood that came along with marrying and establishing one's own household. The fullness of a man's civil and political
status appeared in his becoming an independent head of a unit that included dependents, in his heading a household unit that deserved representation in the polity.

The act of 1855 relied on these principles. It gave the male citizen
greater privileges, and did so by limiting his wife's choice, by making
his wife's and children's nationality derivative of and dependent on his.
It made sure, a congressional sponsor said, that "by the act of marriage
itself the political character of the wife shall at once conform to the political character of the husband." Foreign-born wives of American citizens were deprived of the exercise of independent political consent—or
more exactly, I should say, the act prescribed that consent *to marriage* was
the basic and definitive act of political consent available to them. The
congressional sponsor of the bill saw no infringement or impairment of
rights in it. Implicitly equating political rights with the vote, he presumed that "women possess no political rights." The bill was in his view
simply "a relief to the husband, it aids him in the instilling of proper

---

10. Okin, *Women in Western Political Theory;* Carole Pateman, *The Sexual Contract*
(Stanford: Stanford University Press, 1988).

11. Thomas Jefferson to Edmund Pendleton, August 26, 1776, quoted in Joan Gun-
dersen, "Independence, Citizenship, and the American Revolution," *Signs* 13, no. 1 (au-
tumn 1987): 64. The connections between male headship of a family, property owning, and
citizenship in public policy can be seen quite explicitly in the Jacksonian-era federal
treaties with Indian tribes: U.S. government treaties with Cherokees in 1817 and 1819, for
instance, gave land grants to (male) heads of families who wished to become U.S. citizens;
the treaty of 1830 likewise stipulated that "each Choctaw head of a family being desirous
to remain and become a citizen of the States, shall be permitted to do so, by signifying his
intention to the agent within six months . . . " Quoted in Kettner, *Development of Citizenship,* 292–93.

principles in his children and cannot interfere with any possible right of a political character"—because women had none.[12] Controverting the traditional understanding that Justice Story had articulated in *Shanks v. Dupont*, the bill amplified the common-law doctrine of coverture—the doctrine that a woman, upon marriage, ceded her legal individuality as well as her property to her husband. Such amplification was remarkable in an era when state legislation seemed to be beginning to unseat coverture, with the passage of acts enabling married women to keep title to their property and increasing statutory grounds for divorce.[13]

The second aspect of the 1855 provision that I want to highlight is its racial specificity. Not every woman married to an American citizen was to become an American national—only those "who might lawfully be naturalized under existing laws." This phrase was inserted by Senate amendment to the original House proposition.[14] It was a racial qualification. To be "lawfully naturalized" is to embrace (and to be allowed by the state to embrace) a legal fiction of rebirth into a new nativity, to mimic the citizen who belongs to the national community by birth.[15] When Congress had determined American naturalization policy in 1790 (as the new Constitution gave it power to do), it had stipulated that only "free white persons" could be naturalized. Perhaps more remarkable,

12. *Congressional Globe*, 33d Cong., 1st sess. 13 January 1854, 169–71. Francis B. Cutting of New York sponsored the bill. U.S. congressmen were aware that Britain had already made a similar double move: Parliament in 1844 had passed legislation declaring that foreign-born women marrying British citizens gained British nationality and also confirming British citizenship in the children of British fathers—and mothers—abroad. Cutting had "not gone to that extent" (that is, to include mothers as authors of citizens). On consent, see Carole Pateman, "Women and Consent," *Political Theory* 8, no. 2 (May 1980): 149–68.

13. Although the principle involved was ominous, in practice, the women who gained American citizenship by the 1855 act were mostly glad of it—"not one in a thousand objects," declared a U.S. agent when confronted with one who did, vociferously; quoted in Bredbenner, "Toward Independent Citizenship," 18–20, discussing the case of Elise Lebret protesting her inadvertent loss of French citizenship. On married women's property acts and on divorce in the antebellum era see, for instance, Norma Basch, *In the Eyes of the Law: Women, Marriage and Property in Nineteenth-Century New York* (Ithaca, N.Y.: Cornell University Press, 1982); Richard H. Chused, "Married Women's Property Law, 1800–1850," *Georgetown Law Journal* 71, no. 5 (June 1983): 1359–1425; Norma Basch, "Relief in the Premises: Divorce as a Woman's Remedy in New York and Indiana, 1815–1870," *Law and History Review* 8, no. 1 (spring 1990), 1–24; Glenda Riley, *Divorce: An American Tradition* (New York: Oxford, 1991).

14. The Senate Committee on the Judiciary at first wanted to eliminate the section granting citizenship to wives, but on second thought amended it. *Congressional Globe*, 33d Congress, 2d session, 20–21 December 1854, 8 February 1855, 91–92, 116, 632.

15. On naturalization as a legal fiction, see Kettner, *Development of Citizenship*, 41–43.

this racial exclusiveness became a fundamental tenet of American naturalization policy without any debate. As reported in the *Annals of Congress*, the debate on the 1790 law gave no attention to this limiting phrase. Two of the three senators on the committee delegated to draft the law were from slaveholding states, Virginia and South Carolina, which in their state constitutions had limited naturalization to free white persons. The committee's draft contained the limiting phrase and no one in the Senate contested it—although debate about the proper length of residency for citizenship raged.[16]

The requirements for naturalization named those strangers most clearly welcomed and signaled who would belong most "naturally" to the imagined national community.[17] The wives who were welcomed into the American polity in 1855, then, were free white wives. In 1870, after the Civil War and the Thirteenth and Fourteenth Amendments, Congress extended naturalization privileges to Africans and their descendants, mainly in response to the strenuous efforts of Sen. Charles Sumner. Sumner put a proposal before Congress to remove *all* racial restrictions from naturalization policy, but that proposal failed, because of western senators' animus against the Chinese immigrants who were becoming more numerous in the western states at this time.[18]

After 1870, because whites and persons of African descent could be "lawfully naturalized," the law of 1855 regarding wives' nationality applied to women of both of those groups. A federal circuit court decision in 1898 confirmed that a black woman born in Canada became an American citizen through her marriage to an African-American man. Although native Americans could not be naturalized (they could become American citizens by treaty arrangement), another decision in that decade even interpreted the reach of the 1855 act to mean that a native American woman who had married a white American, left her tribe, and

---

16. *Annals of Congress*, 1st Cong., 2d sess. (1790), 1057, 1109–25.

17. See Benedict Anderson, *Imagined Communities*, rev. ed. (London and New York: Verso, 1991), 5–7, on the concept of the nation as an imagined (limited and sovereign) political community.

18. *Congressional Globe*, 41st Cong., 2d sess., 2 July 1870, 4 July 1870, 5114–25, 5148–77; George M. Fredrickson, *White Supremacy: A Comparative Study in American and South African History* (New York: Oxford University Press, 1981) 145; Edward P. Hutchinson, *Legislative History of American Immigration Policy* 1798-1965 (Philadelphia: University of Pennsylvania Press, 1981), 57–61; James Harrison Cohen, "A Legal History of the Rights of Immigrant Aliens in the United States under the Fourteenth Amendment to the Constitution, 1870 to the Present" (Ph.D. diss., New York University, 1991), 27.

"adopted the habits of civilized life" thereby became an American citizen.[19]

No Asian woman could acquire U.S. citizenship by operation of the 1855 statute. The Chinese population in America hardly worried about a surplus of marriageable women, however—quite the opposite. Among Chinese residents in the United States, who numbered more than 100,000 by 1880, the sex ratio was drastically skewed toward men. It was possibly the most skewed of any immigrant group at any time in the nation's history.[20] Chinese male laborers had first immigrated to follow the gold rush in California in the late 1840s and then were recruited as cheap labor to build the transcontinental railroad (which was completed in 1869). Their presence fueled the prejudices and anxieties manifest in the 1870 naturalization debate. Anti-Chinese feeling soon ballooned into enactments to exclude, first, Chinese prostitutes, and then all Chinese laborers from the United States. The Chinese exclusion acts of 1882, 1892, 1902, and 1904 not only closed Chinese immigration down to a trickle of specific categories of merchants, ministers, and students, but also reaffirmed that Chinese could not become citizens via naturalization.[21]

---

19. Broadis v. Broadis, 86 Fed. 951 (1898); Hatch v. Ferguson, 57 Fed. 959 (1893). The latter decision (about the native American woman) was based on the 1855 statute, even though a subsequent federal law had more direct impact, namely, an act of 1888 declaring that every woman member of any Indian tribe in the United States (except the five so-called "civilized tribes") who thereafter married a citizen of the United States would become a citizen herself, by marriage. See Frederick Van Dyne, *Citizenship of the United States* (Rochester, N.Y.: Lawyers' Cooperative Publishing, 1904), 121. Passage of this law had more to do with Congress's wish to keep white men from claiming exemption from U.S. jurisdiction by marriage to Indian women than it did with desire to make citizens of Indian women.

20. Bill Ong Hing, *Making and Remaking Asian America through Immigration Policy, 1850–1990* (Stanford: Stanford University Press, 1993), 48; Megumi Dick Osumi, "Asians and California's Anti-Miscegenation Laws," in *Asian and Pacific American Experiences: Women's Perspectives*, ed. Nobuya Tsuchida (Minneapolis: Asian/Pacific American Learning Resource Center and University of Minnesota, 1982), 8.

21. There is an excellent concise summary of the nineteenth-century welcome and then enmity for the Chinese and the passage of Chinese exclusion laws in Hing, *Making and Remaking*, 20–26. On Chinese exclusion, see also Hutchinson, *Legislative History*, 67–84, 104, 130, 431–33; and Sidney Kansas, *U.S. Immigration Exclusion and Deportation and Citizenship of the United States of America*, 2d ed. (Albany and New York: Matthew Bender, 1940), 4–6. The very first restrictive immigration law, in 1875, prohibiting the entry of prostitutes and contract laborers, was aimed at Chinese in both categories. See Hing, *Making and Unmaking*, 23, and Sucheng Chan, "The Exclusion of Chinese Women, 1870–1943," in *Entry Denied: Exclusion and the Chinese Community in America, 1882–1943*, ed. Sucheng Chan (Philadelphia: Temple University Press, 1991), 105–9.

The aim to keep Chinese immigrants out of the American body politic was further realized, subtly, by the act of 1855: not so much by its failure to include Chinese women who might marry American men as by its threat to American women who might marry Chinese men and permit them to father Chinese-American citizens. The act of 1855 (and its generous confirmations in state and federal courts), clearly indicating that a woman was one with her husband if he had American nationality, said absolutely nothing about the converse—the American woman who married a foreigner. Did she lose her U.S. citizenship by marrying "out"? Cases on this question were being decided, in less than consistent fashion, during the decades when the Chinese Exclusion Acts were formulated and strengthened.[22] In one leading case of the 1880s in federal court, the judge noted with satisfaction that "legislation upon the subject of naturalization is constantly advancing towards the idea that the husband, as the head of the family, is to be considered its political representative, at least for the purposes of citizenship, and that the wife and minor children owe their allegiance to the same sovereign power." He found it appropriate "to apply the same rule of decision to a case where a female American citizen marries an alien husband, that we should to a case where an alien woman marries an American citizen."[23] In another leading federal case of the 1890s, the judge felt exactly the opposite, concluding that the act of 1855 "was not intended as a general enactment upon the consequences of marriage between people of different nationalities."[24] The inconsistent decisions in these cases meant that the strong possibility of loss of citizenship loomed over any American woman who would marry a Chinese man. Thus discouraging interracial marriage, federal marriage policy backed up the spirit of laws passed between 1861 and 1913 in Arizona, California, Idaho, Montana, Nebraska, Nevada, Utah, and

---

22. On the indeterminacy on the question whether an American woman who married a foreigner lost her citizenship in the years 1855–1907, see Luella Gettys, *The Law of Citizenship in the United States* (Chicago: University of Chicago Press, 1934), 113–19; Van Dyne, *Citizenship*, 127–41; Ernest J. Hover, "Citizenship of Women in the United States," *American Journal of International Law* 26 (1932): 703–40; Waltz, *Nationality of Married Women*, 31–33, Sapiro, "Women, Citizenship," 7–8; Bredbenner, "Toward Independent Citizenship and Nationality," 55–70. See digest of cases confirming the 1855 statute in *Century Edition of The American Digest: A Complete Digest of All Reported American Cases from the Earliest Times to 1896*, vol. 10, 13–15.

23. Pequignot v. Detroit, 116 Fed. 211 (1883), at 216, 214.

24. Comitis v. Parkerson et al., 56 Fed. 556 (1893), at 562.

Wyoming, which made marriages between Chinese and whites criminal and void.[25]

In 1907, Congress ended indeterminacy on the question of American women who married foreigners by passing legislation that expressly followed through the logic of coverture in the 1855 statute. The new law, part of congressional streamlining of immigration and naturalization provisions, declared "that any American woman who marries a foreigner shall take the nationality of her husband." Where in 1855 Congress had invited U.S. men to absorb and replace the national identity of the women of other groups, the 1907 statute forcefully warned American women that they would become aliens in their own country if they married outsiders. This congressional prescription for wives' allegiance passed at the very height of immigration: about a million immigrants per year entered the United States in 1905, 1906, and 1907. It meant not only that American women were discouraged from marrying immigrants by the threatened loss of their own nationality, but also that any immigrant wife could not make her own decision to become naturalized; only if her husband (assuming that he was also foreign-born) sought naturalization could she become an American citizen. And the act had a clear racial cast: the American woman who married an Asian would remain an alien for the duration of her marriage, since her husband could not be naturalized.

By punishing American women who would introduce foreign racial or ethnic elements into the body politic, the 1907 act served a purpose similar to that of state antimiscegenation laws, which criminalized or nullified marriages between whites and persons of color. The 1907 act did not criminalize marriage to an immigrant, even to an Asian, but made the female partner in such a marriage give up her attachment to her country. Losing one's American citizenship meant more than a change of passport or a symbolic punishment. Aliens were not only placed outside the American political community, but also were hampered by material restrictions on occupational choice in many states and, most broadly, on the freedom to own, inherit, and devise property.[26]

---

25. For a summary of laws prohibiting whites from marrying persons seen as belonging to other races, see David H. Fowler, *Northern Attitudes towards Interracial Marriage: Legislation and Public Opinion in the Middle Atlantic and the States of the Old Northwest, 1780–1930* (New York and London: Garland, 1987), appendix.

26. On common-law prohibition of aliens owning, devising, and inheriting property, see Kettner, *Development of Citizenship*. The clear trend during the late nineteenth century

Congress passed this legislation with very little discussion, because of congressmen's assumptions about a woman's essential nonentity once married. Proponents said that the provision was merely "declaratory," that it codified the existing state of the law, that a woman's nationality followed that of her husband. Although such comments overlooked the actual conflicts and controversy in the case law, no congressman was sufficiently well informed or bold enough to say so.[27] The 1907 act showed how far congressmen took the primacy of male citizenship and headship of the family for granted and assumed in corollary that wives' primary political allegiance was to their husbands, not to their country. The contrast between national treatment of male citizens who married foreigners (their wives accepted into the fold—provided they were racially acceptable), and female citizens who married foreigners (themselves and their children ejected from the national community) could not have been more stark.

Yet the 1907 legislation coincided with a rising political trend entirely opposite in meaning—that is, the new percolating vigor and string of successes in the woman suffrage movement. By 1915, when the constitutionality of the 1907 act came before the U.S. Supreme Court, women were enfranchised in a dozen states. Ethel Mackenzie, an American woman who had married an Englishman, was prevented from registering to vote in California (where women were enfranchised in 1911) on the grounds that she was not a citizen. She fought this determination in court, contending that Congress could not take away the birthright nationality of a citizen, as the 1907 legislation purported to do. The U.S. Supreme Court was regrettably unsympathetic to her point of view. By-

---

was to eliminate restrictions of this sort, but many still remained in the early twentieth century; see Richard R. Powell, *Powell on Real Property,* rev. ed. by Patrick Rohan, vol. 1 (New York: Matthew Bender, 1993), 100–109. It is true, too, that during the nineteenth century a number of (underpopulated) midwestern and western states enfranchised aliens who had declared their intent to become citizens although this latitude was widely challenged by the end of the century. See J. B. Raskin, "Legal Aliens, Local Citizens: The Historical, Constitutional, and Theoretical Meanings of Alien Suffrage," *University of Pennsylvania Law Review* 141, no. 4 (April 1993), 1391–1470.

27. *Congressional Record,* 59th Cong., 2d sess, 21 January 1907, 41:1463–67; 27 February 1907, 41:4116; 28 February 1907, 41:4263–64. The act did provide that upon the husband's death his widow could resume her citizenship, and that if she did, her minor children born abroad would become citizens upon taking up residence in the United States. Note that in an earlier discussion of a (failed) bill to allow the American widow or divorced wife of a foreigner to regain her citizenship, senators also assumed that any married woman's nationality was the same as her husband's. *Congressional Record* 58th Cong., 3d sess., 14 January 1905, 39:829–31.

passing the precedent of *Shanks v. Dupont,* and embracing the "ancient principle" of "the identity of husband and wife," the court noted the important fact that the Expatriation Act of 1868 enabled Americans to divest themselves of national allegiance voluntarily. The court further contended that since the 1907 law had warned Ethel Mackenzie of the consequences, her marriage to a foreigner must be judged "as voluntary and distinctive as expatriation."[28]

Punitive as the Supreme Court decision against Ethel Mackenzie seemed, it followed congressional directives to the letter. The Mackenzie case in 1915 caused a good deal more public commentary—and public outrage—than the passage of the act in 1907 had. Shortly afterward, World War I aroused further public awareness of the 1907 provisions, for a number of American-born women who happened to be married to German immigrants were declared enemy aliens and therefore had their property seized.[29] In the woman suffrage movement, where several leading figures, such as Harriot Stanton Blatch, Inez Milholland, and Crystal Eastman, were married to foreigners, the notion that marriage should decide a woman's political capacities was anathema. Suffragists equally rejected the premise that marriage to a foreigner should constitute expatriation and the provision that marriage to an American should constitute citizenship. The demand for equal suffrage required women, married or not, to be regarded as political individuals. Suffragists were horrified that marriage, in its interaction with nationality, could enfranchise some women and disenfranchise others.

It is not surprising, then, that one of the first and most unanimous moves of organized women after the passage of the Nineteenth Amendment was to challenge the provisions of 1855 and of 1907—to eliminate consequences of marriage for women's citizenship.[30] The initial result

---

28. Mackenzie v. Hare, 239 U.S. 299 (1915), 311, 312. Supreme Court Justice McKenna was either ignorant or crafty in declaring that "the identity of husband and wife is an ancient principle of our jurisprudence. . . . It was neither accidental nor arbitrary. . . . It has purpose, if not necessity, in purely domestic policy; it has greater purpose and, it may be, necessity, in international policy," for this claim ignored the precedent of *Shanks v. Dupont,* in which Justice Story said that the political rights of femes coverts, meaning "their acquiring or losing a national character," "do not stand upon the mere doctrines of municipal law . . . but stand upon the more general principles of the law of nations" (248).

29. Waltz, *Nationality of Married Women,* 12–13; Bredbenner, "Toward Independent Citizenship," 67–68, 117–18.

30. J. Stanley Lemons, *The Woman Citizen: Social Feminism in the 1920s* (Urbana: University of Illinois Press, 1973), 63–68, 235–37, includes a brief and helpful overview of the women's movement to achieve "independent citizenship" and the Cable Act's provisions.

of their efforts was the Cable Act of 1922 (named after its congressional sponsor, John Cable). Although some women lawyers had been agitating on the issue since the early 1910s, the enfranchisement of women made all the difference to the passage of the Cable Act. A Massachusetts congressman conceded during congressional debate that once women got the ballot, the existing relation between women's marriage and citizenship became "as archaic as the doctrine of ordeal by fire."[31]

The Cable Act asserted the principle of "independent citizenship" for married women, but it accomplished that only partially. First, it overruled the act of 1855, removing the foreign-born woman's privilege of gaining U.S. citizenship simply by marrying an American man. Instead, such wives were given a streamlined naturalization opportunity: they would have to wait only a year, rather than the standard five years, before going through naturalization procedures, and they could bypass the stage of declaring intent. Second, the Cable Act overruled the Act of 1907 by allowing an American woman who married a foreigner to retain citizenship. Rather than going the simple route of making her marriage irrelevant to or truly independent of her citizenship, however, the Cable Act awarded the American woman married to a foreigner the status of a naturalized citizen, who, if she lived for two years in her husband's country or five years in any foreign nation, was presumed (as any naturalized citizen in that situation was presumed) to have given up her American nationality. In superseding the provisions of 1907, the Cable Act also enabled an immigrant woman married to a noncitizen to apply for naturalization on her own.

Thus undoing the earlier laws, the Cable Act still retained male privilege in citizenship in connection with marriage. Sharp distinctions persisted between the prerogatives of American male citizens who married "out" and American female citizens who did so. Congress did not consider the possibility that foreign-born spouses of American women should have their paths to naturalization cleared. Not only did the American woman not gain any special privileges for her husband, but her own hold on her citizenship was not absolute; rather, it was depen-

---

31. See debate on the Cable Act in *Congressional Record*, 67th Cong., 2d sess., 1922, 62, pt. 9:9039–67; quotation from Rogers on 20 June 1922, 9047. On 1910s efforts, see Bredbenner, "Toward Independent Citizenship," 96–97; and Senate Committee on Immigration, *American Citizenship Rights of Women: Hearing before a Subcommittee of the Committee on Immigration*, 72d Cong. 2d sess., 2 March 1933.

dent on her residence, which was crucially tied to her husband's domicile. On the other hand, the prejudice that an American man should be able to control and decide his wife's nationality—that, whomever he married, his should be a fully *American* household—held strong sway among congressmen. Once the Nineteenth Amendment passed, this prejudice was countered by many congressmen's fears that the dispensation of 1855 would catapult foreign-born women married to American men into unseemly power as voters. The tug-of-war between these two prejudices resulted in the compromise that foreign-born wives of American citizens would have to be resident one year and would have to pass through naturalization procedures to become citizens.[32]

If the Cable Act was about the principle of independent citizenship, why these complications? Why did it not simply emancipate citizenship from marriage considerations completely?[33] The limitations in the law showed how deeply it was embedded in the gender order and the racial order, displaying not only congressmen's (and presumably their constituents') attachments to male citizens' prerogatives, but also the intensifying public hostility toward immigrants, especially those seen as racially unassimilable. Besides the Chinese exclusion laws I have mentioned, immigration was further regulated by Congress in 1891, 1903, 1907, and 1910; in 1917 the Chinese exclusion acts were extended to virtually all of Asia; restrictions leaped forward in the Quota Act of 1921 (first limiting immigrants by country of origin) and culminated in the law of 1924 (the basic provisions of which lasted until 1952).

This movement toward restriction, at its height in the early 1920s when the Cable Act was also passed, was fueled by fear on the part of white Americans of English and northern European stock that the

---

32. The special contribution of Sapiro's article, "Women, Citizenship and Nationality," was to point out that congressmen's anti-immigrant animus was essential to passing the Cable Act. On political efforts before and around the passage of the Cable Act, see Bredbenner, "Toward Independent Citizenship," 127–35. Much earlier, Sophonisba P. Breckinridge, *Marriage and the Civic Rights of Women* (Chicago: University of Chicago Press, 1931), 33–34; and Waltz, *Nationality of Women*, 47 recognized that the Cable Act retained elements of "family unity"—that is, remnants of patriarchal control of citizenship. Another sex discrimination in the act was its providing explicit means for an American woman to renounce her citizenship upon marriage to a foreigner, should she wish to, before any court with jurisdiction over naturalization; the act contained no assumption that a male should or might want to do so; Waltz, *Nationality of Married Women*, 44.

33. Earlier-tried, more egalitarian versions of an independent citizenship bill did not make progress in Congress: see Bredbenner, "Toward Independent Citizenship," 119–27.

"true" American type was being overrun and outpeopled, that American standards of life and work were being undercut by swarthy and non-Protestant hordes from the Mediterranean, Russia, and parts of the world even less known or trusted. The 1921 and 1924 immigration restriction acts drastically lowered the ceiling on all immigration and established maximum quotas for groups by national origin, mimicking the ethnic makeup of the United States *before* the great waves of immigration of 1880 to 1920. The 1924 act barred foreigners who could not be naturalized from even entering the country. Now Asians overall, not only Chinese laborers, were inadmissible, as well as ineligible to citizenship.[34]

It was this last provision, in conjunction with marriage policy, that caught Ng Fung Sing. She had been born an American citizen, but her marriage to a Chinese man made her, in the eyes of American law, Chinese. That was so even though she married in 1924, after the passage of the Cable Act. She was not able to retain her citizenship because the exclusionary sentiments so prominent in the period built into the Cable Act a racial prejudice: American women who married foreigners "ineligible for citizenship" (those who did not meet the racial requirements for naturalization) missed the grant of "independent citizenship" and were treated as under the act of 1907.[35] And if the woman herself did not meet the requirement for naturalization, her marriage made her an alien for life. When Fung Sing arrived in Seattle in 1925, immigration authorities regarded her (because of her marriage to a Chinese and her residence in China) as a Chinese subject, despite her American birth, and therefore ineligible for naturalization and inadmissible into the country. She was a widow, which would ordinarily have meant that her husband's nationality no longer affected her own citizenship—but the Immigration Act of 1924 also had a provision saying that "an immigrant born in the U.S. who has lost his U.S. citizenship shall be considered as having been born in the country of which he is a citizen or subject." This

---

34. On the making of the 1924 law, see Hutchinson, *Legislative History,* 484–85. The history of immigration restriction to 1924 has been detailed by many historians; see (besides Hutchinson, *Legislative History*) Kansas, *U.S. Immigration Exclusion;* and John Higham, *Strangers in the Land: Patterns of American Nativism, 1860–1925* (New York: Atheneum, 1963).

35. All treatments of the Cable Act note this discrimination, including Lemons, *Woman Citizen,* 67; Cyril D. Hill, "Citizenship of Married Women," *American Journal of International Law* 18 (1929): 727; Waltz, *Nationality of Married Women,* 43–44.

provision operated especially harshly against those of Chinese or other Asian descent and seemed exactly designed to keep a woman such as Ng Fung Sing from her American birthright once she had left the country and married a Chinese man.[36]

The racial prejudice in the Cable Act had a direct and particular impact on the Chinese and Japanese populations in the United States. In Asian-American communities, there were American-born adults who had citizenship because they were born on American soil.[37] Yet if an American-born woman of Asian descent married a first-generation Asian immigrant (which was very likely because of the skewed sex ratio), the Cable Act stipulated that she lost her American citizenship.[38] Nor could she regain it, being herself racially ineligible for naturalization.

It was also because of the clause excepting marriage to "aliens ineligible for citizenship" in the Cable Act that Mary K. Das became a woman without a country. Her husband had been naturalized during a period when a number of Hindus, Sikhs, and Parsees managed to do so, on the reasoning that natives of India were ethnologically classified as Aryan or Caucasian and therefore fit the requirement of "free white persons." But in 1923 the U.S. Supreme Court, putting the definition of the Caucasian race aside, decided that Indians were not "white" in the common understanding of that term as used in 1790 and 1870. The decision followed one from the year before, declaring Japanese people likewise ineligible. As the U.S. Supreme Court interpreted the 1790 naturalization statute, its "intention was to confer the privilege of citizenship upon

---

36. *Ex parte Fung Sing;* Waltz, *Nationality of Married Women,* 46.

37. The jus soli, or "right of the soil," as an American tradition stemmed from British practice that birth in the Crown's dominion made one a British subject. The principle was not formally enunciated in the United States until the Fourteenth Amendment to the Constitution (1868), however. In *U.S. v. Wong Kim Ark,* 165 U.S. 649 (1898), a divided Supreme Court affirmed that the child born of Chinese parents on American soil was an American citizen.

38. Chan, "Exclusion," 128–29; Osumi, "Asians," 15–16. Osumi claims that the "aim [of this clause of the Cable Act] was to discourage Nissei [second-generation Japanese immigrant] women and women of other races from marrying Issei [immigrant-generation] men." He points out that in 1920, 42 percent or more of the Japanese men over age fifteen were unmarried. According to Hing, *Making and Unmaking,* 55, the sex ratio among the Japanese population in the United States at that time was almost 2 to 1 (down from 7 to 1 in 1910 because the Gentleman's Agreement of 1907 allowed wives and children of Japanese men already in the country to enter); the sex ratio among the Chinese population was nearly 7 to 1, down from 14 to 1 in 1910 (presumably by natural increase).

that class of persons whom the fathers knew as white" and to deny it to others.[39] Retroactive application of the Supreme Court decision deprived Taraknath Das of his citizenship—which for ten years he had believed valid—and the Cable Act deprived his wife of hers. When she and members of the National Woman's Party, whom she enlisted in her cause, lobbied Congress for amendments to the Cable Act on this issue, she reported bitterly that "some Representatives and Senators, members of the Immigration Committees of the two houses of Congress, hold that the ideal of Americanism should keep any American woman from marrying any foreigner, particularly an Asiatic."[40]

During the House debate on the Cable bill, a couple of congressmen had noted the sex discrimination involved in thus punishing an American woman, while an American man who married an Asian woman kept his citizenship. The best response that John Raker of California, a strong proponent, could muster, was to say, "The man has always had his right of citizenship. The men have dominated the thing from the beginning." When a Kentucky congressman offered an amendment extending the loss of citizenship to men who married aliens ineligible for citizenship by naturalization, it was handily rejected.[41] To serve the goal of that was clearly intended in the making of the immigration laws of 1921 and 1924, congressmen had no trouble reading American woman out of the polity for straying, but they balked at restricting the freedom of American men to choose wives. It was just at this time, in 1923, that

---

39. U.S. v. Bhagat Singh Thind, 361 U.S. 204 (1923), at 208, quoting Takao Ozawa v. U.S., 260 U.S. 178 (1922).

40. Mary Das married in 1924, after the decision in *U.S. v. Thind*. She consulted lawyers as to whether she might lose her citizenship by the marriage and was assured by "experts, one a former adviser to the State Department," that a U.S. Supreme Court decision would never have retroactive effect. Das, "Woman Without," 105–6; Wold, "Woman Bereft"; Cohen, "Legal History," 42–52; Bredbenner, "Toward Independent Citizenship," 289–91. The justification for the effect of *Thind* on Indians naturalized years earlier was that the naturalization had been illegal and void. Cf. "Moves to Revoke Hindu's Citizenship," *New York Times*, 22 September 1925, p. 10.

The question of permanence in citizenship or loss of citizenship came up in several different and contradictory ways in connection with the consequences of marriage. Many courts agreed that the U.S. citizenship that a foreign-born woman gained by marrying an American man was permanent: if he died or they were divorced, she remained a citizen. But an American woman who became an alien via marriage could regain her American nationality after divorce or her husband's death (unless she was "ineligible for citizenship" by naturalization). This happened automatically under the statute of 1907 and via a year's wait and naturalization procedure under the Cable Act.

41. *Congressional Record*, 67th Cong., 2d sess., 20 June 1922, 62, pt. 9:9057, 9063–64.

a U.S. Supreme Court opinion first articulated the right of the individual "to marry, establish a home and bring up children" as a Fourteenth Amendment liberty.[42] The principle that American male citizens ought to be able to create, sustain, and keep together the families they chose was an extremely important one in national thinking and in immigration policy—so important that it vied with and sometimes triumphed over the racialized nationalism of the period. Indeed, the creation of a class of "nonquota" immigrants amid the restrictive act of 1924 was to satisfy this principle. In the Quota Act of 1921, there had been no such class. During the few years that the Quota Act was in force, an American man who married outside of the country could bring his wife home only if she fit under the quota of her country of origin. This affront to the male citizen's right to unite his family caused so much furor and disbelief that a "nonquota" category of admissibles—namely, the wives and children of American male citizens—was established in 1924. Women citizens did not get the right to bring their foreign husbands home to the United States outside of the quota at that time, however. That took another four years of lobbying and an amendment in 1928.[43]

Nor did Asian-American men receive the usual prerogatives of male citizens and husbands. The immigration act of 1924 made special provisions for the entry into the United States of citizens' wives, but it also prohibited admission of persons ineligible to citizenship. What happened when someone was both? The U.S. Supreme Court in 1925 declared, in a case concerning Chinese women married to American-born citizens of Chinese ancestry, that the racial limits on admissibility governed. The men in this case, though American citizens, could not have their wives join them. Chinese-American men lobbied the congressional immigration committees for years before an amendment to

---

42. Meyer v. Nebraska, 262 U.S. 390 (1923).

43. Nor were American women who had lost their citizenship by marriage between 1907 and 1922 allowed to enter outside the quota: they had to reenter the country as quota immigrants in order to move toward regaining their citizenship through naturalization! Waltz, *Nationality of Married Women*, 47; Bredbenner, "Toward Independent Citizenship," 151–55, 203–06, 221–22, 235–40. Note that the first Quota Act (1921) did give male citizens' family members first preference under the quota; these family members had preference above the husbands of American citizens and above American women who had lost their citizenship through marriage and wanted to return to become naturalized. I am indebted to Bredbenner's work for stressing the conflict between the principles of "family unity" and of immigration restriction in the 1920s.

the Cable Act answered them: in 1930, Chinese wives of American citizens who had been married before 1924 were given a special dispensation to enter the country.[44]

Unlike some narratives of policy change, this one has a upbeat ending. As a result of pressure brought by constituents, Congress amended the Cable Act in 1930, 1931, and 1934 until women's citizenship was fully separate from marriage consequences, including the differential consequences of marrying an "alien ineligible for citizenship." The National Woman's Party, the originator of the Equal Rights Amendment and a group sometimes criticized by historians for its elitism, led this effort.[45] While its position was gender-based—focusing on the unfairness of an American woman losing her citizenship for marrying an ineligible alien, when an American man did not—the result achieved was antiracist. It wasn't until 1947, following wartime alliance between the United States and China and postwar occupation of Japan, that all racial barriers excluding citizens' spouses from entering the country were lifted. Five years later, the McCarran-Walter Act eliminated racial barriers to citizenship, substituting new political restrictions instead.[46]

Accomplished because of insistent pressure from interested parties who stressed the injustice of the existing laws, the congressional moves in the 1930s to equalize married women's citizenship with married men's and the formal elimination, in the postwar years, of racial categories of citizenship, took fuller cognizance of individual rights without limits by sex or race than had the earlier policies. The values informing conceptions of justice can and do change, so that, as Justice Thurgood Marshall proposed in an opinion of 1985 (on a different issue), "what once was a 'natural' and 'self-evident' ordering later comes to be seen as an artificial and invidious constraint on human potential and free-

---

44. Chang Chan et al. v. Nagle, 268 U.S. 346 (1925); Breckinridge, *Marriage and Civil Rights*, 31–32; Chan, "Exclusion," 125-26; Bredbenner, "Toward Independent Citizenship," 247–52, 256–57. The 1930 law was quite limited in its coverage, not extending to all Chinese wives of American citizens, only those married before 1924. Bredbenner notes that the wives at issue in *Chang Chan* were still in the United States, on bond, when the reform law passed in 1930.

45. On the 1930s amendments, see Waltz, *Nationality of Married Women*, 51–58; Breckinridge, *Marriage and Civil Rights*, 39–40; Hover, "Citizenship of Women," 718–19; Blanche Crozier, "The Changing Basis of Women's Nationality," *Boston University Law Review* 14 (1934): 129–53; Bredbenner, "Toward Independent Citizenship," 339–40, 473–79; Cohen, "Legal History," 42–52.

46. Cohen, "Legal History," 42–52; and see Robert A. Divine, *American Immigration Policy, 1924–1952* (New Haven: Yale University Press, 1957), 146–76.

dom."[47] Yet to conclude that the policy changes on citizenship and immigration were dictated strictly by enlarging conceptions of justice to the individual would be naive and would ignore the relation of these changes to assessments of domestic order and to congressmen's assumptions about the role that the United States was destined to play in international politics as the leader of the "free" world.[48] Conceptions of justice in national policy are never separate from conceptions of national interest. If either shifts, so may the other. The reformation of citizenship and immigration policy that took place in the mid-twentieth century can be appreciated without it suggesting that the earlier chapter is so removed from the present day that it can be forgotten—not while shades of racial and gender hierarchy still tinge the policy landscape.

---

47. City of Cleburne v. Cleburne Living Ctr., Inc., 473 U.S. 432 (1985), at 466, quoted in Andrew Koppelman, "The Miscegenation Analogy: Sodomy Laws as Sex Discrimination," *Yale Law Journal* 98 (November 1988): 165.

48. See Divine, American Immigration Policy, 146–76.

Freedom, Equality, Pornography

Joshua Cohen

Equality and Expressive Liberty

According to Andrea Dworkin, "The left—ever visionary—continues to caretake the pornography industry, making the whole wide world— street, workplace, supermarket—repellent to women."[1] Dworkin is right that many people who locate themselves on the political Left oppose restrictive pornography regulations.[2] Her explanation of this opposition is uncertain, however, because she does not explain what she means by "the left." Let's assume, then, that it refers to people whose

This chapter began as a reply to a talk at Brown University by Catharine MacKinnon on "Pornography: Left and Right" (March 1993). I presented a draft in my fall 1993 Political Philosophy seminar at MIT and later versions at Wesleyan University, McGill University Law School, and the Central Division meeting of the American Philosophical Association (spring 1995). I am grateful to those audiences, and to Cass Sunstein and Pam Spritzer, for helpful criticisms, and to Karen Rothkin for research assistance.

1. "Women in the Public Domain: Sexual Harassment and Date Rape," in *Sexual Harassment: Women Speak Out*, ed. Amber Coverdale Sumrall and Dena Taylor (Freedom, Calif.: Crossing Press, 1992), 3. This passage restates a central message of Dworkin's earlier writing on pornography: that the Right's celebration of domesticity and the Left's celebration of sexual liberation represent two variations on the same malign themes—a practice of male dominance, an ideology of male supremacy, and a metaphysics of women as whores. See Andrea Dworkin, *Pornography: Men Possessing Women* (New York: Penguin, 1981), 203–9.

2. The American conflict over pornography regulation has parallels elsewhere, for example in British debate in the early 1990s. For debate among British feminists, see Catherine Itzin, ed., *Pornography: Women, Violence, and Civil Liberties* (Oxford: Oxford University Press, 1992); Feminists Against Censorship, *Pornography and Feminism: The Case Against Censorship*, ed. Gillian Rodgerson and Elizabeth Wilson (London: Lawrence and Wishart, 1991); Lynne Segal and Mary MacIntosh, eds., *Sex Exposed: Sexuality and the Pornography Debate* (London: Virago Press, 1992).

conceptions of justice give a large place to social equality—everyone who accepts, at a minimum, the following propositions:

1. Substantive equality of opportunity is a basic element of social justice. Substantive equality of opportunity—as distinct from the formal equality of opportunity associated with the ideals of equality before the law and careers open to talents[3]—requires that people not be disadvantaged in life because they were, for example, born with few resources, with dark skin, or female.
2. Existing inequalities of wealth and power thwart substantive equality of opportunity.
3. Achieving substantive equality of opportunity requires an affirmative role for the state—for example, in regulating market choices. For "if inequality is socially pervasive and enforced, equality will require intervention, not abdication, to be meaningful."[4]

This understanding of the Left is quite comprehensive, encompassing virtually all egalitarians. Precisely for this reason it highlights the interest and polemical thrust of Dworkin's point. For more than a decade now, one group of feminists has urged pornography regulations as a strategy for combating the erotization of sexual subordination, arguably an important factor in reproducing sexual inequality.[5] Egalitarians embrace regulations of "market choices" in the name of economic equality and commonly accept certain regulations of political expression—the content-neutral regulation of political expenditures—in the name of political equality.[6] In short, they emphasize the importance of liberty and equality as political values, accept regulations of choice in

---

3. On the distinction, see John Rawls, *A Theory of Justice* (Cambridge: Harvard University Press, 1971), sec. 12; Brian Barry, *Theories of Justice* (Berkeley: University of California Press, 1989), secs. 26–28.

4. Catharine MacKinnon, "Privacy v. Equality: Beyond Roe v. Wade," in her *Feminism Unmodified: Discourses on Life and Law* (Cambridge: Harvard University Press, 1983), 100.

5. On equality as the basis for pornography regulation, see Catharine MacKinnon, *Only Words* (Cambridge: Harvard University Press, 1993), part 3. On feminist opposition to pornography regulation, see Nadine Strossen, *Defending Pornography: Free Speech, Sex, and the Fight for Women's Rights* (New York: Scribner, 1995), 31–5.

6. See John Rawls, "The Basic Liberties and Their Priority," in *Political Liberalism* (New York: Columbia University Press, 1993), lecture 8, secs. 7, 12; Charles Beitz, *Political Equality* (Princeton: Princeton University Press, 1989), chap. 9.

the name of equality, and in some areas (say, the economy) think that justice requires such regulation. If substantive equality of opportunity is an important aspect of justice, and if there are background inequalities of power between men and women, then why, apart from reflex appeals to freedom of speech, resist the regulation of "sexual choices" in the name of sexual equality?[7]

One answer is that the regulations are divisive and diversionary, and probably ineffective cures for subordination. Although such pragmatic objections carry some weight, they fail to account for the special energy that has surrounded the debate about regulation—a debate that has focused on rights of expression. Moreover, for reasons I will discuss later, the Left—as I have interpreted Dworkin's use of the term—cannot rely exclusively on such objections. According to a second line of argument, stringent regulations of pornography are wrong, and not just unlikely to be effective.[8] I think these criticisms have some force, and I propose to explore its scope and limits.

More specifically, I make three principal points:

1. The debate about pornography regulation, like much American political debate, is excessively legal.[9] We are invited, for example, to assume that the MacKinnon-Dworkin account of pornography is correct, then asked to consider what can we do about it, consistent with taking the First Amendment seriously.[10] As a matter of method, I suggest that

---

7. "The law of equality and the law of freedom of speech are on a collision course in this country." MacKinnon, *Only Words*, 71.

8. The regulations favored by MacKinnon and Dworkin are civil, not criminal, and it might therefore be said that they are not "stringent." But stringency should not be settled by reference to regulatory form; it depends on the extent of a regulation's coverage and the sanctions attached to violating it. Restrictions on political speech prior to *New York Times v. Sullivan* were stringent, though they derived from tort law.

9. For a striking and interesting exception, see Susan E. Keller, "Viewing and Doing: Complicating Pornography's Meaning," *Georgetown Law Journal* 81: 2195–2228. See also Nadine Strossen, *Defending Pornography*. Strossen's book, published after I completed the penultimate draft of this chapter, argues that pornography regulations conflict with settled First Amendment doctrine and that they would be bad for women's rights and equality, both because their enforcement would likely be damaging to women and because they rest on distorted views of women (as victims), sex (as degrading to women), and pornography (as uniformly negative about women). Although I dislike the book's polemical tone and cartoonishly simple picture of the First Amendment, I agree with much of its content and with Strossen's effort to engage the substance of sexual expression and not simply its doctrinal status.

10. The classic version of this strategy of argument is Judge Easterbrook's opinion in *American Booksellers Ass'n. v. Hudnut*, 771 F.2d 323 (7th Cir. 1985), affirmed without opinion, 475 U.S. 1001 (1986).

the argument—even the legal argument—ought to be more about pornography. The proper resolution of issues about regulation depends on what pornography is and whether it merits the strong protections properly extended to political and artistic expression or rather the reduced levels of protection appropriate to commercial speech or personal libel.[11] An assessment of pornography regulation can no more avoid a discussion of the interests implicated in sexually explicit expression than an account of commercial speech regulation can proceed without reference to the interests implicated in it.

2. Because sexual expression serves basic interests, regulations of the sort advanced by MacKinnon and Dworkin are unacceptably broad and intrusive. Egalitarians ought not to treat the ideas of sexual choice and sexual liberation simply as ideologies that reflect, mask, and sustain practices of sexual subordination. I sketch a more limited form of pornography regulation—targeted on constitutionally obscene materials that sexualize violence (the pornographically obscene)—that is less vulnerable to objection than more restrictive regulations. But its restricted range is bound to limit its impact.

3. People committed to an ideal of justice that embraces substantive equality and expressive liberty ought not simply to notice the lack of substantive equality, express opposition to restrictions on expression, and conclude with hand-wringing about the shame of sexual inequality and how sadly tragic it is that a commitment to liberty stands as a bar to its remedy. We need to find a way to accommodate both commitments. So I conclude by sketching some proposals that might accommodate commitments to equality and free expression.

To put the main idea in broader terms: From Emma Goldman to Noam Chomsky, an important strand of the egalitarian tradition has urged that expressive liberty is an intrinsic element of human liberation and a precondition for popular democratic politics. I endorse that strand of free-speech egalitarianism and explore its implications for the case of pornography.

A Rationale for Regulation

In this section, I sketch one style of argument for regulation, drawn largely from Catharine MacKinnon. So there is nothing original in the

---

11. On reduced protection of commercial speech, see C. Edwin Baker, *Human Liberty and Freedom of Speech* (Oxford: Oxford University Press, 1989), chap. 9; Rawls, "The Basic Liberties," 363–68.

substance of my presentation, though I have tried to make the argument's assumptions and logic fully explicit.[12]

1. As a general matter, women suffer systematic social disadvantage by comparison with men. They are economically subordinate, required to bear the double burdens of production and reproduction, and physically insecure and subject to abuse.[13]

2. Such systematic disadvantage—that is, sexism—is a fundamental injustice. Like racism, it makes a difference into a source of disadvantage, violating the requirement of substantive equality of opportunity.

3. The reproduction of unjust, systematic disadvantage—whether the distinction underlying the disadvantage is sex, race, or class—is always a complicated causal story, featuring the internalization of dominant norms, social formation of desires that fit with existing opportunities, and rational calculations of advantage under constraints. But force, and threats of force, are also part of the answer. In the case of gender, women are subject to abuse by men, to rape, incest, harassment on the street and at work, physical abuse at home. Such violence and pervasive threats of violence have a social function. Not merely the sick behavior of individual men, they serve as enforcement mechanisms, as disciplinary devices that contribute to the reproduction of a system in which sex is a basis for disadvantage by increasing the costs to women of violating gendered norms of proper behavior.[14]

---

12. For an especially clear statement of these themes and their connections, see Catharine MacKinnon, "Pornography as Defamation and Discrimination," *Boston University Law Review* 71 (1991), 795–802. She emphasizes (at 796): (1) that women are "used, abused, bought, sold, and silenced," (2) that "this condition is imposed by force," and (3) that "pornography has a central role in actualizing this system of subordination in the contemporary West." My presentation in the text aims to fill out these three points and make the connections more explicit. Also, see Catherine Itzin, "Pornography and the Social Construction of Sexual Inequality," in Itzin, *Pornography*, chap. 2; Wendy E. Stock, "Feminist Explanations: Male Power, Hostility, and Sexual Coercion," in *Sexual Coercion: A Sourcebook on its Nature, Causes, and Prevention*, ed. Elizabeth Grauerholz and Mary A. Koralewski (Lexington, Mass.: Lexington Books, 1991), 61–73.

13. On abuse, see MacKinnon, *Only Words*, 7. More generally, see, for example, Susan Faludi, *Backlash: The Undeclared War Against American Women* (New York: Crown, 1991); Susan Okin, *Justice, Gender, and the Family* (New York: Basic Books, 1989), chap. 7.

14. On sexual abuse as a disciplinary device, see Duncan Kennedy, "Sexual Abuse, Sexy Dressing, and the Eroticization of Domination," in *Sexy Dressing: Essays on the Power and Politics of Cultural Identity* (Cambridge: Harvard University Press, 1993), 147–62. Wendy Stock summarizes some of the empirical literature linking fear of assault (rape, in particular) with ("self-imposed") behavioral restrictions in her "Feminist Explanations," 67.

In short, force and threats of force function as enforcement mechanisms for gender norms, thus helping maintain a system that disadvantages women because of their sex and benefits men because of theirs.[15]

4. Many people—and not only men[16]—find subordination and the force that helps sustain it sexually exciting: they find sexism and its disciplinary armature sexy.[17]

5. An important part of the explanation for the reproduction of sexual subordination is that many people—and not only men—find subordination and the force that helps to sustain it sexually exciting.[18] Because they find sexism sexy, they tolerate—or actively embrace—subordination and violence. In short, sexism is reproduced because it is sexy.

6. It is not original or intrinsic to human nature that people find sexism sexy. Although sexual desire, abstractly understood, may be intrinsic and original,[19] the particular forms of sexual desire dominating our

---

15. Of course the fact of disadvantage—the imbalance of power—also explains vulnerability to the imposition of sanctions. Coercion, then, reflects the vulnerability that it helps sustain. For an interesting and subtle discussion of the issue of male benefit, see Kennedy, "Sexual Abuse," 138–47.

16. "Some [women] eroticize dominance and submission; it beats feeling forced. Sexual intercourse may be deeply unwanted—the woman would never have initiated it—yet no force may be present." Catharine MacKinnon, "Feminism, Marxism, Method, and the State," *Signs* 8 (1983): 650; also MacKinnon, "Does Sexuality Have a History?" in *Discourses of Sexuality,* ed. Domna C. Stanton (Ann Arbor: University of Michigan Press, 1992), 134.

17. Affirming and linking the third and fourth points, Jane Caputi says that rape, like femicide, "is a social expression of sexual politics, an institutionalized and ritual enactment of male domination, and a form of terror that functions to maintain the power of the patriarchal order [point three]. Femicide, moreover, is not only a socially necessary act; it also is experienced as pleasurable and erotic [point four]." Caputi assumes—though she does not say here—that its being experienced as pleasurable and erotic helps explain why it is done, that is, why acts that are "socially [i.e., functionally] necessary" are actually performed (see point 5 in the text). See Caputi, "Advertising Femicide: Lethal Violence Against Women in Pornography and Gorenography," in *Femicide: The Politics of Women Killing,* ed. Jill Radford and Diana E. H. Russell (New York: Twain Publishers, 1992), 205.

18. Whereas point 4 alleges a fact about sources of sexual excitement, point 5 gives prominent place to that fact—as distinct from, say, the sexual division of household labor, or early patterns of socialization, or strategies of human capital investment—in explaining sexual inequality.

19. Nothing in the argument requires affirming (or denying) the naturalness of some form of sexual desire. The distinction between a natural and socially constructed form of sexual desire traces at least to Rousseau. See his *Discourse on the Origin and Foundations of Inequality Among Men,* trans. Victor Gourevitch (New York: Harper and Row, 1986), 163–66.

lives are a product of politics—in particular, the power of men and a culture dominated by that power.[20]

7. Pornography plays a central role in defining what sexuality is for us, in particular in sexualizing—and so making permissible and attractive—subordination and the force that helps to sustain it. It "works by making sexism sexy;"[21] it "makes hierarchy sexy."[22] More strongly put: pornography "is *a major way* [my emphasis] in which sexism is enjoyed and practiced as well as learned."[23]

Pornography, a subset of sexually explicit expression (see the later section "The Regulations" for the legal definition), sexualizes subordination in two ways. First, its content fuses sex and subordination. It presents women as enjoying subordination and as willing subjects of it: resistance as desire; fear and horror as enjoyment; "no" as "yes."[24] By presenting subordination and the abuse that serves to sustain it as consensual, pornography presents them as acceptable: "the victim must look free, appear to be freely acting. Choice is how she got there."[25]

---

20. Strossen badly misunderstands MacKinnon's views on this point. She says that "procensorship feminists," including MacKinnon, believe that men are "essentially bestial" (*Defending Pornography*, 113). It is difficult to understand how a reader of MacKinnon's work could think that MacKinnon believes that men or women are *essentially* anything. For example: "Sometimes people ask me, 'Does that mean you think there's no difference between men and women?' The only way I know how to answer that is: of course there is; the difference is that men have power and women do not. I mean simply that men are not socially supreme and women subordinate by nature; the fact that socially they are, constructs the sex difference as we know it. I mean to suggest that the social meaning of difference—in this I include *différance* [sic]—is gender-based" ("Desire and Power," in *Feminism Unmodified*, 51). Strossen offers a misinterpretation of a passage from MacKinnon's *Only Words* as supporting evidence.

21. MacKinnon, "Pornography as Defamation and Discrimination," 802.

22. MacKinnon, "Pornography, Civil Rights, and Speech," *Harvard Civil Rights—Civil Liberties Law Review* 20 (1985): 17.

23. MacKinnon, "Pornography as Defamation and Discrimination," 796. John Stoltenberg puts the point still more strongly: "Pornography is what makes subordination sexy" [my emphasis]. See his "Gays and the Pornography Movement: Having the Hots for Sex Discrimination," in *Men Confronting Pornography*, ed. Michael Kimmel (New York: Crown Publishers, 1990), 260.

24. The experimental literature on the effects of exposure to violent pornography in particular appears to bear out this claim about the importance of presenting women as "willing victims." In experimental settings, men who are not antecedently angry at a woman (the confederate in the experiments) are then exposed to a rape video in which the victim expresses pleasure at the end. They are more likely to be aggressive with the confederate in subsequent stages of the experiment than men who are exposed to a rape video in which the woman is said to find the experience humiliating and degrading. See Edward Donnerstein, Daniel Linz, and Steven Penrod, *The Question of Pornography: Research Findings and Policy Implications* (New York: Free Press, 1987), 98.

25. Catharine MacKinnon, "Frances Biddle's Sister," in *Feminism Unmodified*, 172.

Moreover, by presenting them as sexually exciting—as what sex is—it has the effect of fusing sexual desire with the desire for relations of subordination and domination: it accounts for the distinctive, politically constructed content of sexual desire. "In the subordination of women, inequality itself is sexualized: made into the experience of sexual pleasure, essential to sexual desire. Pornography is the material means of sexualizing inequality; and that is why pornography is a central practice in the subordination of women."[26] Pornography produces a psychology perfectly suited to a social structure of sexual inequality, and in so doing provides the linchpin for the reproduction of such inequality.[27]

How precisely does pornography produce such a psychology? How, in Dworkin's words, does it sexualize "inequality itself" and serve as the "material means of sexualizing inequality"? Two mechanisms—one cognitive, the other behavioral—have been proposed to account for this fusion. The cognitive mechanism reflects the fusion of sexuality and subordination in pornographic images, the background fact of male dominance, and two psychological facts—that we grasp concepts in part by mastering their paradigmatic instances and that our desires are, as a general matter, concept dependent. According to this proposal, men master the concept of sex (and related concepts, including sexual pleasure, enjoyment, satisfaction, gratification) in part by recognizing the enjoyment of force and subordination as sexual enjoyment. Given a background of male power, these pornographic paradigms of sexuality are generalized: "Men treat women as who they see women as being. Pornography constructs who that is. Men's power over women means that the way men see women defines who women can be. Pornography is that way."[28] Suppose, now, that desires are concept dependent, that we cannot specify the content of desires independently from the concepts available to the person whose desires they are—that, as applied to the case of sex, our sexual desires are desires for sex as we socially cognize it. As a result, sexual desires themselves are desires for sexual subordination; what counts as and what is experienced as sexual enjoyment reflects the pornographic conception of sexuality: "feminism exposes

---

26. Andrea Dworkin, "Against the Male Flood," in *Pornography*, 527.

27. I suspect that adherents of the view sketched in the text implicitly assume that such a close fit between structure and psychology is required for the reproduction of sexual inequality. But there are many reasons, short of full endorsement, for compliance with, or consent to, a system of inequality. For one discussion of such reasons, see Joshua Cohen and Joel Rogers, *On Democracy* (New York: Penguin, 1983), chap. 3.

28. Catharine MacKinnon, "Not a Moral Issue," in *Feminism Unmodified*, 148.

desire as socially relational, internally necessary to unequal social orders but historically contingent."[29] The problem in short is not that guys are animals or that they never grow up; the trouble lies in the perfection of their (our) socialization under conditions of sexual inequality.

According to the behavioral mechanism, pornography works by "conditioning men's orgasm to sexual inequality."[30] Pornography depicts subordination and force; men watch (or read or listen to) pornography; they masturbate; that reinforces an association between sexual excitement and subordination (alternatively, men and women together watch, read, or listen to pornography; they have sex; that reinforces a link between male sexual excitement and subordination). MacKinnon suggests an important role for this behavioral mechanism when she distinguishes the contribution of pornography to sexual inequality from the contribution of racial hate speech to racial subordination. Whereas pornography "manipulates the perpetrator's socialized body relatively primitively and directly," and works "by circumventing conscious processes,"[31] "[n]othing analogous to the sexual response has been located as the mechanism of racism, or as the mechanism of response to sexist material that is not sexual."[32] These claims are puzzling. If the distinction ("nothing analogous") is simply that racist hate speech does not work through sex, then it seems uncontroversial, but irrelevant. If the distinction assumes that racist hate speech works through conscious processes, then it is of clear relevance, but highly implausible, and at odds with common understandings of categorization and stereotyping.[33] In any case, the behavioral mechanism is less plausible because it

---

29. Catharine MacKinnon, *Toward a Feminist Theory of the State* (Cambridge: Harvard University Press, 1990).

30. MacKinnon, "Pornography as Defamation and Discrimination," 802. It is not clear in this article whether MacKinnon endorses the behavioral mechanism described in the text; it is more strongly suggested in her *Only Words*, 16. Diana E. H. Russell provides the clearest statement in "Pornography and Rape: A Causal Model," in *Pornography: Women, Violence, and Civil Liberties*, ed. Catherine Itzin (Oxford: Oxford University Press 1992), 324. Also, see Stoltenberg, "Pornography, Homophobia, and Male Supremacy," in ibid, 148.

31. Several proponents of pornography regulation have argued that its direct effects on the body, unmediated by cognition, remove it from the category of protected expression. For discussion and criticism, see David Coles, "Playing by Pornography's Rules: The Regulation of Sexual Expression," *University of Pennsylvania Law Review* 143, no. 1 (November 1994): 124–27.

32. See MacKinnon, *Only Words*, 61–62.

33. See, for example Henri Tajfel, *Differentiation Between Social Groups: Studies in the Social Psychology of Intergroup Relations* (London: Academic Press, 1978).

applies only to men whose orgasms are associated sufficiently frequently with consuming pornography for the reinforcement to work its effects.

An Excursus

This account of pornography derives its force from its apparent fit with certain illustrative cases of pornography. Consider, for example, *Shackled*, a quarterly magazine published by London Enterprises Limited "in the interest of informing and educating the adult public on the various forms and means of sexual expression."[34]

Shackled is, as the name indicates, a bondage and discipline magazine, one of roughly thirty-five such magazines distributed by Lyndon Distributors. More precisely, it is a bondage and discipline magazine depicting women bound and disciplined (men are presented through their words, not in pictures). The work of "informing and educating the adult public" starts with the cover: one issue features a naked woman lying on her back with her legs spread, eyes closed, a ball-gag in her mouth, and wrists in leather cuffs, which are strapped to the metal bed she is lying on. Another woman stands behind her, checking the strap that holds the ball-gag in place. The cover line reads, "Girls Who Love Heavy Restraint! See 'Em Stripped Naked and Chained." A page 2 editorial—which includes the language about "informing and educating"—tells us that "Finding girls who love heavy restraint is easier than folks imagine. The censors who seek to ban bondage magazines—like this one—should understand that these are girls who enjoy shackles." The first photo layout ("Bi-Babe Bondage") features two women, "One who thrives on suffering and tight restraint, the other on dishing out pain." Another shows a woman (the girlfriend of a "brilliant young barrister" who has brought her to the "bar of justice") with her wrists attached to a metal bar (said bar), eyes blindfolded, and mouth taped. According to the caption: "The tighter the rope—and the bigger the dick—the better she likes it." Another: "Sure it hurts my tits, but I enjoy every pang." Another: "Steel cuts into her tit, a gag into her mouth, but does she complain? Hell, yes!" The last layout: "Heavy chain and padlocks are her special thing. The weight really turns her on." And it concludes: "After an hour of bondage, she's screaming for hard cock."

---

34. Editorial, *Shackled*, no. 9 (May 1993): 2.

It does not add up to much of a narrative, but it covers the major points. Sexualize subordination ("girls stripped naked and chained"). Emphasize the moment of consent: that these women love enforced subordination (that it is easier to find bondage lovers than you might have thought, that they "love heavy restraint," "enjoy shackles," "thrive on suffering and restraint," and "thrill to that constricting feeling, whether from rope or metal"). Depict pain and resistance as part of the pleasure, and so as constituting no objection to subordination ("thrives on suffering," "Sure it hurts my tits, but I enjoy every pang"). Finally, link subordination, the bondage that enforces it, and the consent that legitimates bondage (the pleasures of the accompanying pain) with intercourse and male orgasm ("The tighter the rope—and the bigger the dick—the better she likes it"). Thus the slogan: "pornography makes sexism sexy."

No Other Exit

I return later to *Shackled*. For now, let's consider the argument for regulation, which falls out more or less directly from the analysis I sketched earlier. Not simply an argument about the "themes" or "ideas" present in pornography, the case turns principally on claims about what pornography does: "Men treat women as who they see women as being. Pornography constructs who that is. Men's power over women means that the way men see women defines who women can be. Pornography is that way."[35] Operating through the cognitive and behavioral mechanisms, pornography makes subordination and the force that contributes to its reproduction sexually exciting and definitive of women's nature: it gives sexual desire and the experience of sexual satisfaction—which are not intrinsically attracted to subordination—their determinate content;[36] it gives subordination a central role in our self-definition as men and women ("Gender is sexual"[37]); and it makes the harm of enforced subordination "invisible as harm" by presenting women as consenting to and enjoying their own subordination and abuse.[38]

Suppose all of this is right. Then, pornography is *key to making sex-*

---

35. MacKinnon, "Not a Moral Issue," 148.
36. MacKinnon, "Pornography as Defamation and Discrimination," 802.
37. MacKinnon, "Not a Moral Issue," 148.
38. MacKinnon, "Francis Biddle's Sister," 178; also MacKinnon, *Feminist Theory of the State*, 204.

ual subordination into a system—to "creating and maintaining sex as a basis for discrimination."[39] Pornography serves as a linchpin not simply because of what it says, but because of what it does.[40] It takes our sexuality, a deep fact about our lives, and enlists it—as idea, identity, desire, and practice—in support of subordination. Pornography is not a treatise that justifies subordination, but a device that makes it seem right, look natural, and feel good. By producing a psychocultural setting that makes us experience sexism as irresistible, it closes off all avenues of exit from subordination, except the avenue of regulating pornography itself.

This account of pornography's role is sometimes summarized in the claim that pornography subordinates—and not simply that its graphic, sexually explicit depictions of subordination *cause* subordination to be sexualized. A pornography ordinance adopted in Indianapolis in 1984 defines pornography in part as "the graphic sexually explicit subordination of women, whether in pictures or in words" (for the full definition, see the next section, "The Regulations"). "What pornography *does* goes beyond its content: it eroticizes hierarchy, it sexualizes inequality. It makes dominance and submission into sex."[41] The claim that pornography subordinates should be understood in three ways.

1. The production of pornography regularly uses force.[42]
2. Sexual force against women sometimes involves the use of pornography as a model: men force women to view pornography and to do what the pornography shows women doing.

---

39. Minneapolis Public Hearings, cited in Donnerstein, Linz, and Penrod, *Question of Pornography,* 139.

40. MacKinnon, *Only Words,* 22.

41. MacKinnon, "Francis Biddle's Sister," 172; MacKinnon, *Only Words,* 11, 22. For proposals about how to interpret the claims that pornography subordinates and silences, see Rae Langton, "Speech Acts and Unspeakable Acts," *Philosophy and Public Affairs* 22, no. 4 (fall 1993): 293–330; Andrew Altman, "Liberalism and Campus Hate Speech: A Philosophical Examination," *Ethics* 103 (January 1993): 302–17.

42. As MacKinnon emphasizes, the claim that some pornography is made using coercion is not the "legal basis for restricting all of it" (*Only Words,* 20). Still, the pornography industry appears especially sensitive to the charge that coercion and abuse are central to the production of pornography. This sensitivity is highlighted in the Code of Ethics adopted by the Free Speech Coalition (an industry association). Five of eight items in the code address issues about the consensual nature of the production of pornography (including one that condemns the use of drugs and alcohol in production and another that requires performers to be old enough to give their consent). See *Adult Video News* 8, no. 7 (June 1993): 24. On the extent of force in production, see Strossen, *Defending Pornography,* chap. 9.

3. Pornography reproduces sexual inequality by shaping gender identities and sexual desires in ways that make force attractive, subordination natural, and their injuries invisible. Given male power, pornography has those effects; and once those effects are in place, the reproduction of sexual inequality is the inevitable result.

I offer these three points as explication of the claim that pornography *is* "the graphic, sexually explicit subordination of women." But do they really explain the *"is"*? I have two responses: "yes" and "wrong question."

As to "yes": what I have described is *how*—according to defenders of regulation—pornography subordinates: by depicting subordination and force as sexy, thereby giving sexual desires and gender identities their content. Consider an analogous case. Suppose I say to you, "I didn't incite the people demonstrating in front of the building to burn the building down; I simply urged them to do it, and by urging them caused them to be incited to burn it down." To which the right response is: "You are telling me *how* you incited them, not that you didn't."

Similarly with subordinating: suppose someone says, "I know there is subordination, that pornography depicts subordination and violence as sex, that it thereby makes subordination and violence sexually exciting, and that subordination is reproduced because it is experienced as gender identity and sexual desire. But the pornography does not subordinate." It is perfectly fair for the critic to respond thus: "You have told me how it subordinates; not that it doesn't."

As to "wrong question": I think it is a mistake to suppose that the issue of regulation can or ought to be settled by first determining whether pornography is expression that *says* something objectionable and thereby *causes* injury or instead *is* injurious conduct (perhaps an illocutionary speech act)—put otherwise, by first determining whether it causes subordination or subordinates.[43] This supposition reflects a gen-

---

43. For discussion of speech act theory and pornography, see Langton, "Speech Acts." According to Langton, pornography subordinates (and silences) only if pornographers' speech is authoritative about matters of sex (311). I cannot see how this could settle the issue, because their speech may be authoritative because people regard them as "in the know" and so listen to them. Or it might be that men who think that women enjoy subordination go to pornography to learn how to do it (not because a producer of pornography is in authority, but because he or she is an authority). No amount of speech act theory is going to shift the debate away from causal argument and questions about the assignment of responsibility.

eral approach to freedom of expression that exaggerates the importance of a prior expression-action distinction in settling issues of regulation.[44] An answer to the expression-or-action question is, I think, not best understood as a premise in argument about the regulation of expression. We do not first decide "expression or action" and then decide whether to regulate. Rather, the distinction reports a conclusion: when we have decided that regulation is permissible, we say that expression is conduct—we say that when we have decided to assign responsibility to the speech (think of blackmail and extortion). When we think regulation is inappropriate—when we are reluctant to assign responsibility to the use of words, rather than to events downstream—we say that the words are speech. But it is wrong to think that we settle the "speech or action?"/"saying or doing?" antecedent to argument about the assignment of responsibility and the permissibility of regulation and then use that resolution in deciding the regulatory issue.

As applied to the issue at hand: the disagreement about whether pornography is subordinating conduct or is instead speech that may cause subordination is best understood as a disagreement about whether regulation is appropriate. It is best understood as a disagreement about where to assign responsibility, not as a claim about causation or constitution that might resolve an argument about such assignment.

The Regulations

Pornography regulations—for example, the ordinance adopted in Indianapolis in 1984 and overturned in 1986—reflect this analysis. The Indianapolis ordinance defines pornography as:

> The graphic sexually explicit subordination of women, whether in pictures or in words, that also includes one or more of the following:
>
> - Women are presented as sexual objects who enjoy pain or humiliation;

---

44. For criticism of the project of founding an account of freedom of expression on a prior expression-action distinction, see Thomas J. Scanlon, "A Theory of Freedom of Expression," *Philosophy and Public Affairs* 1 (1972): 205–8.

- Women are presented as sexual objects who experience sexual pleasure in being raped;
- Women are presented as sexual objects tied up or cut up or mutilated or bruised or physically hurt;
- Women are presented being penetrated by objects or animals;
- Women are presented in scenarios of degradation, injury, torture, shown as filthy or inferior, bleeding, bruised or hurt in a context that makes these conditions sexual;
- Women are presented as sexual objects for domination, conquest, violation, exploitation, possession, or use, or through postures or positions of servility or submission or display.[45]

The regulations establish four offenses: coercing someone into pornographic performance, forcing pornography on a person, assault caused by "specific pornography," and trafficking in pornography. They empower an administrative agency to issue cease-and-desist orders against those who commit these offenses and to award damages to victims. And, whereas offenses under the coercion, forced viewing, and assault provisions cover materials in each of the six categories described in the regulation, the trafficking provision covers only the first five. The intent of this limit is to confine the trafficking provision to more violent and hard-core pornography.[46] But not all materials that fall into the first five categories are violent or brutal. Susie Bright's anatomically precise discussion of the many varieties of dildo in her "Shiny Plastic Dildos Holding Hands" appears to fall into the fourth category, because women in it are penetrated by objects. But the depiction is neither violent nor brutal.[47] For now, though, let's put such details to the side.

To see the connection with the analysis of the injuries of pornography, consider the contrast with obscenity regulations. In the 1973 case of *Miller v. California*, the Supreme Court held that expression is obscene

---

45. Indianapolis, Ind., City-Council General Ordinance No. 35 (June 11, 1984). The full text is cited in MacKinnon, *Feminism Unmodified*, 274 n. 1. The regulation was overturned in *American Booksellers Ass'n. v. Hudnut*.

46. Owen Fiss, for example, describes the materials covered by the trafficking provision as "the most violent and brutal forms of pornography." See his "Freedom and Feminism," *Georgetown Law Review* 80, no. 6 (August 1992): 2051.

47. See Susie's Bright's *Sexual Reality: A Virtual Sex World Reader* (Pittsburgh and San Francisco: Cleis Press, 1992), 27–36. Consider, too, the sexual fantasies involving animals reported in Nancy Friday, *Women on Top* (New York: Simon and Schuster, 1991), 106–11, 444–45. The passages reporting these fantasies appear also to fall into the fourth category.

and so has a reduced level of First Amendment protection only if it is offensive, prurient, and of no serious literary, artistic, political, or scientific value: in short, offensive, sexually preoccupied, crap.[48] Pornography regulations differ from obscenity regulations on each of these three dimensions.

1. Pornography regulations do not go after the prurient.[49] Their target is not sexual explicitness, preoccupation, or perversion but graphic materials that sexualize subordination. The concern is not—or at least is asserted not to be—pornography's sexual content, but its role in discrimination.

2. The regulations are not justified by reference to the *offensiveness* of graphic subordination[50]—nor because it insults, damages reputations of women as a class,[51] or inspires disgust, guilt, or fear[52]—but by the harms of such representations, their role in reproducing a system of discrimination that turns the fact of sexual difference into a basis for social inequality.

The concern with the harm of sexual subordination is less immediately in evidence with the coercing, forcing, and assault provisions, which target either uncontroversially harmful consequences (assault) or coercive means (coercion and forced viewing). Such injuries are substantial, quite apart from their implications for discrimination. But even in these cases, the regulations reflect a concern with subordination: why target, for example, the forced viewing of pornography rather than all forced viewing, or coerced performances in pornography rather than all coerced performances? The natural explanation is that the aim is to remove, or at least to chill the production and distribution of, materials that fall into these six categories—materials that subordinate. Although the trafficking provision, then, is the most controversial element of the regulations, it reveals their overall aim, which is to target materials that sexualize subordination, not simply those that produce specific injuries associated with particular uses of pornography.

48. See Miller v. California 413 U.S. 15 (1973).
49. On the problems of showing prurience, see MacKinnon, *Only Words*, 88.
50. Ibid., 100.
51. MacKinnon criticizes the reputational injury view of pornography in "Pornography as Defamation and Discrimination"; see also MacKinnon, *Only Words*, 11.
52. It does seem to inspire such reactions in some women: a survey published in *Cosmopolitan* in March 1990 reported that 66 percent of respondents (all women) did not enjoy seeing pornography, 32 percent felt disgusted, 32 percent felt offended, 31 percent felt guilty, and 18 percent felt frightened. See Catherine Itzin and Corinne Sweet, "Women's Experience of Pornography," in *Pornography: Women, Violence, and Civil Liberties*, ed. Catherine Itzin (Oxford: Oxford University Press, 1992), 228.

3. They allow no exception for materials with serious literary, artistic, scientific, or political value.[53] This distinction connects with an important difference: the natural objection to obscenity regulations is that offensiveness is not a sufficient basis for state regulation. The exemption for materials with serious value provides the basis for a reply: "because this stuff has little value, the normal presumption against regulating offensive expression is suspended."[54] The issue with pornography is different. Harm, unlike offense, does conventionally establish a case for legal regulation—at least outside the context of expression. So, here the question is: given the harms, why does it matter if the stuff is not worthless?

Policy Case against Regulation

Thus the case for regulation. Why doesn't it settle the matter—at least for people who endorse a conception of justice in which equality is an important political value? Equality is a fundamental political value; some uses of state power are justified because they promote that value. So why not in this case? Because pornography regulations violate the right to free expression? Maybe so. But let's put aside reflex appeals to rights of expression—the issue is why we should think those rights are at stake here, and sufficiently so to cause troubles for the regulations.

The Lawyer's Battery

What are the alternatives to a reflex appeal? One is to offer a familiar lawyer's battery of arguments against the regulations:
  • The Case for Regulation is Too Speculative: "I agree that there is subordination [point 1]; that it is a basic injustice [point 2]; that it is maintained in part through force [point 3], which I hasten to add is already illegal; and that some people get off on it [point 4]. But is it so clear that the sexualization of subordination explains much about the reproduction of subordination [doubting point 5]? And if it does—and even acknowledging that sexuality is socially constructed [accepting point 6]—how compelling is the evidence that pornography lies at the heart of that

---

53. "The ineffectualness of obscenity law is due in some part to exempting materials of literary, political, artistic, or scientific value. Value can be found in anything, depending, I have come to think, not only on one's adherence to postmodernism, but on how much one is being paid. And never underestimate the power of an erection, these days termed 'entertainment,' to give a thing value." MacKinnon, *Only Words*, 87–88.

54. On the presumption, see Cohen v. California, 403 U.S. 15 (1971).

construction [doubting point 7]? Even if I grant that the sexualization of subordination is important to sex discrimination, I still have real doubts about whether pornography is the right target.

"Labor market segregation, economic inequality, and the unequal division of the labor of reproduction and socialization are far more important than the sexualization of subordination in explaining the reproduction of subordination. Or if you prefer to concentrate on cultural sources of gender inequality, consider conventional representations of women in commercial advertising. If you want to understand the legitimation of force, consider the pervasiveness of violence in popular culture and *Texas Chainsaw Massacre* and Brian de Palma–style slasher movies. Or if you want to focus on the sexualization of subordination, try the endless sexualization of movies and commercial advertising. Consider, in short, sexism without sex or violence; or violence without sexism or sex; or violent sexism without sex; or sexually suggestive sexism without violence or vivid subordination.

"With so much to consider, why pick on pornography as the basis of sex discrimination? Pornography is, after all, less pervasive than other cultural images, and less believable because it is so highly ritualized, badly written, and poorly acted.[55] Isn't it really because pornography is *sexually explicit*?[56] Isn't the political motive to build an alliance between people who are antisexism and people who are antisex? And so isn't the line between pornography and obscenity regulation really, in the end, not so sharp?"[57]

This last set of polemical questions is meant to suggest that the diagnosis set out earlier is not what drives the focus on pornography. But the more fundamental objection fueling those political suspicions is that the diagnosis is too speculative to sustain the case for regulation.[58]

---

55. See Carlin Meyer, "Sex, Censorship, and Women's Liberation," *Texas Law Review* 72 (1994): 1097–1201.

56. In a discussion of pornography and advertising, Jane Caputi lumps together sexism without sex or violence (an Yves Saint Laurent stocking ad), sexism and violence without explicit sex (Brian de Palma movies), sexism and sex without violence (*Penthouse* magazine), and the combination of sexism, sex, and violence (the movie *Cunt Torture*). According to Caputi, they all have the effect of "reflecting, normalizing, and legitimating violence against women." She does not indicate the regulatory implications of this conclusion. See Caputi, "Advertising Femicide," 203–21. For MacKinnon's response to the question in the text, see her *Only Words*, 61–62.

57. See, for example, Feminists Against Censorship, *Pornography and Feminism*, 28–29. The suggestion there is that the focus on sexual explicitness reflects a strategy of political alliance aimed at winning conservative, antisex allies.

58. See Strossen, *Defending Pornography*, 39.

• Besides, The Regulations Themselves Are too Vague: "Assume, arguendo, that pornography is the linchpin of the system of sexual inequality. Still, the ordinances are hopelessly vague: 'sexual objects who enjoy . . . humiliation'; 'postures or positions of servility or submission or display.' Who could possibly tell whether their work was actionable under such a regulation?"[59]

Consider, for example, Susie Bright's "Story of O Birthday Party." Susie Bright's girlfriend Honey Lee arranges a thirtieth birthday celebration modeled on Pauline Reage's *Story of O*. She dresses Susie Bright in a tight leather corset, has her shine the boots of a policewoman, and arranges for a "gourmet sadomasochist" friend to whip her.[60] Is this pornography, as the regulation defines it?

The story does, to be sure, include humiliation. And while "enjoyment" does not fully capture Susie Bright's response to the humiliation, she does at least partly enjoy it. But it is hard to see Susie Bright as a "sexual *object* who enjoys humiliation," rather than a sexual subject who sometimes enjoys humiliation, or at least who enjoys playing at enjoying humiliation, or enjoys playing at wondering (and getting other people to wonder) whether she enjoys humiliation.

And there are plenty of postures and positions of servility, submission, and display. But do these postures, set within the "Story of O Birthday Party," subordinate? Perhaps not, given the author. Of course they might be said to subordinate *women as a class*, even though they do not subordinate Susie Bright. But why not think instead that because they do not subordinate Susie Bright, they do not subordinate *women as a class*.

Consider, for example, this interchange between Susie Bright and Coral—the gourmet sadomasochist.[61]

SB: How am I supposed to take this pain? It is so intense. I don't
    know where to go with it.
C: When I get hit, I like to think about deserving it, needing to be
    punished.
SB: I can't do that. I was just thinking the very opposite . . . all I can
    think of is that I don't deserve this. I didn't do anything wrong.
C: Well, you can do it for Honey Lee. I know that's what she'd like.

59. Feminists Against Censorship, *Pornography and Feminism*, 69; Strossen, *Defending Pornography*, 75.

60. *Susie's Bright's Sexual Reality*, 17–26.

61. Ibid., 24. I have edited out inessential details and omitted some ellipses.

> SB: Yes, that's what O would do, but I'm too selfish for that.
>
> C: You can be selfish as well. A lot of people like to take the pain, and connect the intensity to their clit or their nipples.
>
> SB: Maybe. When you stroke my clit and fuck me, I appreciate the whip a little, because my cunt sucks the sensation right up.
>
> [Coral hits her twice with the bamboo cane.]
>
> SB: Coral, please, please, I can't do it, please, Jesus, I can't.

After begging Coral to stop, "She complied instantly." And then, as Bright leaves, she says "Coral, you're going to suffer terribly for what you did to me today."

Is this "graphic subordination"? Or graphic insubordination? Does it sexualize subordination? Or make a compelling case that sado-masochistic "herotica" is not for everyone? Perhaps it is and does all these things, depending on the audience. But to introduce this dependence on the audience is precisely to underscore the uncertainty about what the regulations cover.

• Moreover, More Narrowly Drawn Regulations Would Be Pointless: "Assume that the regulations were tightened up—as in the restriction of the trafficking provision to more hard-core and violent materials. As they become narrower and more precise, they become less objectionable. But the less restrictive regulatory means are also less likely to be effective in achieving the stated aim of sexual equality. Moreover, the likelihood grows that other remedies—still less restrictive of expression—will do just as well. So the dangers grow of diverting attention and resources from real cures by focusing on pornography."

• And, Anyway, The State is Patriarchal: "Who can trust the state to regulate speech—in particular to regulate it in ways that serve the interests of women?[62] Consider the parallel with race: a Two Live Crew song was the first target of an obscenity prosecution for a piece of music. Give the state power to regulate expression and it will inevitably use that power on less-powerful citizens.

"Put this well-founded mistrust together with the point about the vagueness in the regulatory language. Do we want—do women want— the state (say, the state of Utah) deciding whether oral sex is a posture of sexual submission?[63] Suppose the man is standing up, and the

---

62. See Burstyn, "Beyond Despair," 158; and Strossen, *Defending Pornography*, 217-46, particularly her discussion of Canadian regulation in the wake of Butler v. the Queen, 1 S.C.R. 452 (1992, Canada).

63. See Feminists Against Censorship, *Pornography and Feminism*, 69.

woman is kneeling. Suppose she is sitting on a chair. What about anal sex? Suppose the woman is on her hands and knees. Suppose she is lying on her back. Suppose she is on her hands and knees, but the anal sex is part of a safe sex video.

"Many distinctions can be drawn, and exploring their nuances makes attractive fare for conferences on cutting-edge film theory.[64] But this is not a role for courts, or for the administrative bodies empowered to hear civil rights complaints under the proposed ordinances, especially given that 'the law sees and treats women the way men see and treat women. The liberal state coercively and authoritatively constitutes the social order in the interest of men as a gender—through its legitimating norms, forms, relation to society, and substantive policies.'"[65]

Limits of the Lawyer's Battery

These considerations all have some force, and I will say later just what that force is. But it is, I believe, commonly exaggerated. Taken on their own, these four points are not especially damaging to pornography regulations, for parallel objections apply to acceptable regulations in other areas (acceptable at least to those who endorse equality as an important political value).

Start with the first claim about speculativeness—that pornography has not been shown to be the problem, so regulations of it may not really get at the harms that they are alleged to address. This point is surely correct. Experimental evidence and cross-national studies fail to establish a compelling case for connections between pornography and rape and subordination. Indeed, most studies find no connection between nonviolent pornography—sexually explicit and sexist—and increased aggression or a heightened disposition toward sexual coercion and violence. There is some evidence for a connection between violent pornography and hostility toward women. Taken together with studies about the effects of graphic, nonsexual violence, however, that evidence suggests that the problem is the violence, not the sex.[66]

But none of these doubts settles anything. The problem with this

---

64. For an interesting discussion of pornography and safe sex videos—delivered at such a conference—see Cindy Patton, "Safe Sex and the Pornographic Vernacular," in *How Do I Look: Queer Film and Video*, ed. Bad Object-Choices (Seattle: Bay Press, 1991), 31–51, and the discussion at 51–63.

65. MacKinnon, *Feminist Theory of the State*, 161–62.

66. For a review of the literature, see Donnerstein, Linz, and Penrod, *Question of Pornography*, esp. chap. 6.

first objection is that many regulations—for example, regulations of economic activity—are not supported by demonstrative reasoning, but only by considerations that do not offend common sense. Maybe the demand for labor really is highly elastic, and minimum-wage laws hurt the poor by shrinking the pool of low-wage jobs. Maybe they do not force firms to enhance productivity by training workers and upgrading technology. Maybe the principal effects of rent control are to limit the supply of housing and generate a secondary market for sublets from long-term renters, worsening the situation for low-income people. People disagree about these issues. But egalitarians believe that democratically elected bodies have the authority to decide how best to ensure substantive equality and to employ strategies based in some measure on speculation.[67] Why, then, prevent democratically elected bodies—like the Indianapolis City Council—from going after abuse and subordination by regulating what they judge to be an essential link in the chain?[68]

We'll get to the second point momentarily, but turn now to the third point—that narrower regulations are less objectionable, but also less likely to succeed. That observation is certainly true. But it is difficult to see how it amounts to a deep objection to the regulations, rather than a familiar policy disagreement.[69]

Or take the final consideration: about mistrust in the state's capacity to regulate speech. Generic mistrust of the state cannot be the reason for opposing the regulation of pornography, at least not for egalitarians. Generic mistrust would reject the affirmative state that, at least in the context of a market economy, is necessary to economic egalitarianism. Whatever the favored methods of ensuring distributive fairness—progressive taxation, support for public schools, programs of training and retraining, regulations on concentrations of wealth—the state has an important role to play in achieving it.

Suppose we narrow the scope of the mistrust, focusing it on the state's capacity to regulate expression. That will not do either. I take it to be common ground among egalitarians that commercial speech ought not to receive the strong protection appropriate to political advo-

---

67. It is not up to them whether to ensure substantive equality: justice demands that.

68. Frank Michelman, "Conceptions of Democracy in American Constitutional Argument: The Case of Pornography Regulations," Tennessee Law Review 56 (1989): 291–322.

69. See Fiss, "Freedom and Feminism," 2052.

cacy: for example, false and misleading commercial representations should not get the same protection as false and misleading political speech.[70] But the state enacts and enforces regulations of false and misleading commercial speech.

It is equally implausible to make the case rest on the refined distinctions that the state would need to draw in order to regulate sexually explicit expression—or, as in the second objection, the vague language of the regulations. Courts must constantly make extremely fine distinctions and interpret vague language. Courts decide if capital punishment is cruel, whether animal slaughter is a legitimate part of a religious practice, which imbalanced agreements are unconscionable, whether twenty-four-hour waiting periods are unduly burdensome on rights of reproductive choice, and which persons are public figures for the purposes of libel law. Why can't they, in the fullness of time, develop ways to determine which postures are servile, for the purposes of adjudication?

But don't all these replies to the objections neglect the fact that what pornography regulations regulate is *expression?* And isn't it appropriate to impose a higher burden of proof on such regulations? It is not the replies that neglect this fact; it is the objections themselves that do. Indeed, that is the point of the replies, which, generically speaking, underscore that the arguments in the lawyer's battery *assume* what needs to be shown: that regulations of pornography must meet a very high burden of justification, a higher burden, for example, than regulations of economic activity or commercial speech or personal libel. Much of the debate about pornography that pretends to assess the evidence for its harmful effects is rather about the proper burden of proof: about how compelling the evidence needs to be. More specifically, criticisms commonly assume a very high burden of justification. Of course, setting the burden very high is almost certain to defeat the regulations (scrutiny of them will be "strict in theory, fatal in fact"): they will be overtaken by concerns about speculativeness, vagueness, the availability of less restrictive alternatives, and mistrust.

But the prior question is whether the burden ought to be pushed so high. Why protect pornography so stringently that the objections in the

---

70. For an argument based more fundamentally on mistrust, see Richard Epstein, *University of Chicago Law Review* 59 (1992): 41–90. For criticisms, see Frank Michelman, "Liberties, Fair Values, and Constitutional Method," *University of Chicago Law Review* 59 (1992): 91–114.

lawyer's battery suffice to defeat regulations? That is the question. And the arguments considered thus far do not answer it. To say this is not to dismiss the four objections, and later I will come back to them, indicating the role that they should play in the rejection of stringent regulations. But first we need to address the more fundamental question.

Stronger Case Against Regulations

What, then, is the problem with pornography regulations? To answer this question, I start with some general background on the basic expressive and deliberative interests that underlie the case for stringently protecting expressive liberty.[71] Then, I develop the following two theses:

1. The same reasons that support stringent protections of, for example, artistic and political expression apply to expression that would be restricted by Indianapolis-style regulations (the same basic interests are at stake here as well).
2. Because those reasons apply, the lawyer's battery does have some force, and therefore it is important to offer other means for addressing the harms of subordination.

Basic Interests

Strong protections of expressive liberty serve three basic interests—expressive, deliberative, and informational—and the weight of those interests explains the importance of especially stringent protections.[72] I have argued for this view elsewhere (see note 71) and will confine my remarks here to a sketch of the expressive and deliberative interests.

---

71. This discussion of the fundamental interests draws on my "Freedom of Expression," *Philosophy and Public Affairs* 22, no. 3 (Summer 1993): sec. 3.

72. Freedom of expression is commonly associated with such values as the discovery of the truth, individual self-expression, a well-functioning democracy, and a balance of social stability and social change. See Thomas Emerson, *The System of Freedom of Expression* (New York: Random House, Vintage, 1971). Lee C. Bollinger emphasizes as well the importance of encouraging tolerance in *The Tolerant Society* (Oxford: Oxford University Press, 1986); and Vincent Blasi examines the role of freedom of expression as a check on official misconduct in "The Checking Value in First Amendment Theory," *American Bar Foundation Research Journal* 3 (1977): 521–649. I think that the tie to the basic interests provides a more fundamental explanation for the protections. For discussion, see Cohen, "Freedom of Expression," secs. 3, 4.

The *expressive* interest is a direct interest in articulating thoughts, attitudes, and feelings on matters of personal or broader human concern, and perhaps through that articulation influencing the thought and conduct of others. Some examples will clarify the nature of the interest and the bases of its importance.

A common feature of different evaluative conceptions is that they single out certain forms of expression as especially important or urgent; the conception implies that an agent has weighty reasons for expression in certain cases or about certain issues. Consider two central cases in which agents hold views that assign them very strong, perhaps compelling, reasons for expression:

1. In a range of cases, the limiting instance of which is a concern to "bear witness," an agent endorses a view that places her under an *obligation* to articulate that view and perhaps urge on others a different course of thought, feeling, or conduct. Restricting expression would prevent the agent's fulfilling what she takes to be an obligation; it would impose conditions that the agent reasonably takes to be unacceptable. Here, expressive liberty is on a footing with liberty of conscience, regulations are similarly burdensome, and the magnitude of the burden reflects the weight of the reasons.

2. In a second class of cases, expression addresses a matter of political justice. Here, the importance of the issue—indicated by its being a matter of justice—provides a substantial reason for addressing it. The precise content and weight of the reason are matters of controversy. According to some views, public engagement is the highest good, and Brandeis urged that "public discussion is a political duty."[73] But even if political expression is neither the highest good nor a matter of duty, still, it is a requisite for being a good citizen, sometimes a matter of sheer decency. Characteristically, then, it has support from substantial reasons within different moral-political conceptions.

Other important cases include an interest in creating things of beauty. But the two I have mentioned suffice to underscore the importance of the expressive interest. They work outward from the case of fully conscientious expression, the paradigm of expression supported by substantial reasons from the agent's point of view. To be sure, different evaluative conceptions have different implications for what is reasonable to say and do. But all conceptions assign to those who hold them

---

73. Whitney v. California, 274 U.S. 357, 375 (1927) (Brandeis, J., concurring)

substantial reasons for expression, quite apart from the value of the expression to the audience, and even if there is no audience at all.

My emphasis on the expressive interest may suggest that the conception of expressive liberty I sketch here is more sectarian than I claim, in particular that it depends on a general philosophy of life according to which self-expression is the fundamental human good. But no such expressivist philosophy is at work.[74] The characterization of the expressive interest focuses on the role of reasons, and that distinguishes it from conventional discussion of the value of self-expression and self-fulfillment. When, for example, people aim to comply with the moral obligations assigned to them by their moral views (whatever the content of those views), it may be misleading to treat their action as a matter of self-expression or self-fulfillment: from the inside, the conduct is mandatory, and the agent may think that conduct important because it fulfills an obligation disconnected from the self's inner nature.[75]

The *deliberative* interest has two principal aspects. The first is rooted in the abstract idea—shared by different evaluative conceptions—that it is important to do what is genuinely worthwhile, not simply what one now believes to be worthwhile. For this reason, we have an interest in circumstances favorable to finding what is worthwhile: that is, to finding out which ways of life are supported by substantial reasons.

The second aspect of the deliberative interest is rooted in the idea that it is important that one's evaluative views not be affirmed out of ignorance or out of a lack of awareness of alternatives. Alongside the interest in doing what the strongest reasons support, then, there is also an interest in understanding what those reasons are and the kind of support they give. This, too, leads to an interest in circumstances favorable to such understanding.

These two aspects of the deliberative interest are connected to expression because reflection on matters of human concern characteristically requires others to advance alternative views. So the deliberative interest calls for circumstances suited to understanding what is worth doing and what the reasons are that support it—for example, circumstances featuring a diversity of messages, forcefully articulated.

---

74. On expressivism, see Charles Taylor, *Sources of the Self: The Making of Modern Identity* (Cambridge: Harvard University Press, 1989), chaps. 21, 24, 25.

75. Kantians will identify acting from the moral law with revealing our nature as free, reasonable beings. Although I do not wish to dispute the truth of that view, I think that a conception of free expression should not depend upon it. For discussion, see Cohen, "Freedom of Expression," 223–24.

Finally, the *informational interest* is an interest in securing reliable information about the conditions required for pursuing one's aims and aspirations. Although sexual expression does advance this interest, it is also less weighty than the others and so I will put it to the side.[76]

Interests and Pornography

I want now to suggest that the problems with stringent regulations lie in their capaciousness. More particularly, they are—both in the underlying principles and in their details—designedly inattentive to the expressive and deliberative interests in the sexually explicit materials that are, by the lights of the regulations, pornographic.

Let's start with the expressive interest. Earlier I mentioned cases of bearing witness and of expression on matters of political justice. In a third class of cases, concerns about human welfare and the quality of human life prompt expression; the evident importance of those concerns provides substantial reasons for the expression.

A paradigm is expression about sex and sexuality—say, artistic expression (whether with propositional content or not) that displays an antipathy to existing sexual conventions, to the limited sensibilities revealed in those conventions, and the harms they impose. In a culture that is, as Kathy Acker says, "horrendously moralistic," it is understandable that such writers as Acker challenge understandings of sexuality "under the aegis of art, [where] you're allowed to actually deal with matters of sexuality."[77] Again in an interview, Kathy Acker says: "I think you'd agree there are various things in us—not all of which are kind, gentle, and tender—readers of de Sade and Genet would probably agree on this point! But I think you can explore these things without becoming a mass murderer . . . without causing *real* damage, without turning to *real* crime. One way of exploring these things is through *art*; there are various ways of doing this. We have . . . to find out what it is to be human—and yet not wreak total havoc on the society."[78]

The human significance of sexuality lends special urgency to the explorations Acker describes. Moreover, that urgency does not decline

---

76. On pornography's informational role, see Strossen, *Defending Pornography*, 165–67.

77. See Kathy Acker, "Devoured by Myths: An Interview with Sylvere Lotringer," in *Hannibal Lecter, My Father* (New York: Semiotext(e), 1991).

78. Kathy Acker interview by Andrea Juno in *Angry Women*, ed. Andrea Juno and V. Vale (San Francisco: Re/Search Publications, 1991), 184–85.

when sexuality mixes with power and subordination—when it is not "kind, gentle, and tender." On the contrary, a writer may reasonably think—as Acker apparently does—that coming to terms with such mixing is especially important, precisely because, in the world as it is, power is so deeply implicated in sexual identity and desire. To stay away from the erotization of dominance and submission is to avoid sexuality as it, to some indeterminate degree, is. But because the proposed regulations address what pornography (allegedly) does, they make no provision for the importance of the expressive interest—for the weight of the reasons that move at least some people to produce sexually explicit materials that conflict with the regulations.

At this point, a proponent of the regulations may wish to concede the point about the expressive interest but wonder why anyone would think that this interest outweighs the harms of pornography. I reply to this concern after first discussing the deliberative interest.

An essay by several members of the Feminist Anti-Censorship Task Force (FACT) suggests the connections between deliberative interests and pornography:

> [The existence of pornography] serves some social functions which benefit women. Pornographic speech has many, often anomalous, characteristics. One is certainly that it magnifies the misogyny present in the culture and exaggerates the fantasy of male power. Another, however, is that the existence of pornography has served to flout conventional sexual mores, to ridicule sexual hypocrisy and to underscore the importance of sexual needs. Pornography carries many messages other than woman-hating: it advocates sexual adventure, sex outside of marriage, sex for no other reason than pleasure, casual sex, anonymous sex, group sex, voyeuristic sex, illegal sex, public sex.[79]

They describe the importance of sexually explicit materials from the audience's point of view, not—as with the expressive interest—from the speaker's, and claim that such materials enable audiences to understand sexual possibilities, perhaps to reconceive their own sexual com-

---

79. Lisa Duggan, Nan Hunter, and Carole Vance, "False Promises: Feminist Anti-pornography Legislation," in *Caught Looking: Feminism, Pornography, and Censorship*, ed. Kate Ellis, Beth Jaker, Nan D. Hunter, Barbara O'Dair, and Abby Tallmer (East Haven, Conn.: Long River Books, 1992), 82.

mitments. And—though the passage just cited does not say this—that enabling is not confined to more kind and gentle erotica; it cuts across the lines drawn in the regulations.

Three features of sexually explicit expression—its diversity, interpretability, and uncertain connections with sexual practice—are important to the connections between sexually explicit materials (including materials covered by pornography regulations) and the deliberative interest.[80]

By "diversity," I mean the sheer variety of pornography. Earlier, I mentioned Shackled, which is illustrative but not representative. There are also many Fem-Dom magazines and videos, featuring dominant women and submissive men (or a mixture of submissive men and submissive women). In fact, one study shows Fem-Dom magazines outpacing Male-Dom.[81] Moreover, bondage and discipline is only one of many themes in contemporary pornography. With easy desktop publishing, low-cost VCRs, and sexual materials all over the Internet, XXX cinemas are in decline and the pornography market is not confined to men in trench coats. The shifting technologies and markets have apparently had important implications for content. There is more bisexual, gay male, lesbian, soft X (no erection, no penetration), and sadomasochism (downplaying genital sexuality), and more heterosexual pornography that is not organized around a culminating cum shot.[82] The fact of diversity baffles efforts to identify a single message of pornography, underscores the "many messages" described in the FACT passage, and suggests that pornography is more than a device that triggers erections and orgasms.

By interpretability, I mean that different viewers/listeners/readers will respond to pornography differently in part because of the wideranging sexual beliefs, feelings, sensibilities, desires, and imaginations

---

80. These points are common in what Judith Butler calls the "pro-sexuality movement within feminist theory and practice." See her Gender Trouble: Feminism and the Subversion of Identity (New York: Routledge, 1990), 30–31; see also Susan Keller, "Viewing and Doing: Complicating Pornography's Meaning," Georgetown Law Review 81 (1993): 2195–2228; Kennedy, Sexy Dressing, 126–213.

81. See Lynne Segal's introduction to Sex Exposed, 6.

82. On the many varieties of pornography, see Linda Williams, "Pornographies on/scene," in Sex Exposed: Sexuality and the Pornography Debate, ed. Lynne Segal and Mary MacIntosh (London: Virago Press, 1972), 233–65; Cindy Patton, "Safe Sex," 31–51; and the interview with "Kay" in Robert Stoller, Porn: Myths for the Twentieth Century (New Haven: Yale University Press, 1991), 120–25. For a striking illustration of market fragmentation, see the list of alt.* newsgroups on the Internet.

they bring to it. There appears to be no hope of establishing a common conception of sexuality or a shared understanding of sexual pleasure and its role in a good human life—for example, of the relative importance of love and release from conventional inhibition in making for good sex. Lacking any basis in a shared, public view about sexuality, interpretations of pornography (and reactions to it) vary widely. Like the fact of diversity, this variation makes it tendentious to suppose that hard-core, sexually explicit expression contains a single message of sexual subordination or has a determinate effect. And the absence of a single message or determinate effect underscores the connections with the deliberative interest.

Let's return to the case of *Shackled*. Earlier, I presented a flat interpretation of it, presenting it as a paradigm of sexualized subordination. But other readings of its message and effect are available. For example, no men appear in the pictures: does this show that phallic absence enhances phallic power, or does it suggest that men are irrelevant to women's sexual pleasure? Moreover, we have a magazine evidently intended for male pleasure, which emphasizes throughout the pleasures of the shackled women. In one interpretation, this emphasis is what erotizing subordination is all about; but perhaps *Shackled* is a gender-bender magazine, the intent or effect of which is to encourage a male audience to identify with the shackled women who are experiencing pleasure; and perhaps the pictorial absence of men is a precondition for fully identifying with the women. Or maybe *Shackled* is about transgression and resistance: after all, is "screaming for hard cock" a matter of begging or commanding? To raise these questions is not to deny the obvious: photographs of women in chains, loving their bondage, and screaming for sex are not likely to do much to reduce sexual subordination or men's apparently inexhaustible reserves of misogyny. But I doubt that a world without *Shackled* will be created by more stringent regulations of pornography or by denying its human complexity.

Finally, the uncertain connections of pornography and practice also weaken the link between pornography and subordination and suggest connections with the deliberative interest. Pornography is as much an ingredient of sexual fantasy as it is a guide to sexual practice. Though some may see it as reflecting or guiding practice, others will see that it provides pleasures in part precisely because it enables viewers/readers/listeners to explore in fantasy (or play) aspects of desire and identity that they do not wish to pursue in practice (the pleasure of pretending to do the forbidden). Moreover, pornography does not simply "advocate" alternatives to conventional sexual practice, but instead it shows—as Duncan Kennedy has argued about sexy dressing—the erotic possibilities that lie in the transgression of conventions: the transgression itself is important to the erotic power.[83]

Commenting on the complex connections of pornography and practice, Susie Bright, for example, reminds us that our fantasies are not "some kind of *McGuffey's Reader* on how to live."[84] And, speaking to the issue of transgression, she adds that the "sexual liberation" message goes further than feminism "in not just *criticizing* the fact that sex roles were restricting, but advocating that sex roles had erotic possibilities if you *subverted* them."[85]

But as this last point underscores, pornography can play a role in advancing the deliberative interest in a world of unequal power in part by engaging our sexual desires, categories, identities, and fantasies as they are—even if our aim is to transform them. On this point, Judy Butler makes an essential observation: "[S]exuality is always constructed within the terms of discourse and power, where power is partially understood in terms of heterosexual and phallic conventions. . . . If sexuality is culturally constructed within existing power relations, then the postulation of a normative sexuality that is 'before,' 'outside,' or 'beyond' power is a cultural impossibility and a politically impracticable dream, one that postpones the concrete and contemporary task of rethinking subversive possibilities for sexuality and identity within the terms of power itself."[86] As applied to the issue of pornography, this proposed "rethinking . . . within the terms of power" suggests that regulations targeted particularly on the fusion of sexuality and subordination—on the apparent extremes of heterosexual and phallic conventions—will cover too much. For it may be in part by working with that fusion and acknowledging its force, rather than by simply depicting a world of erotic possibilities beyond power, that we establish the basis for transforming existing forms of sexuality.

It may be objected, however, that if reflection proceeds *within the terms of power*, then it does not advance the deliberative interest, which

83. "Sexual expression . . . subverts every taboo by making it a fetish. The forbidden is simultaneously eroticized." Cole, "Playing By Pornography's Rules," 116.

84. See the interview of Susie Bright by Andrea Juno in *Angry Women*, 201.

85. Ibid., 202.

86. Butler, *Gender Trouble*, 30.

is an interest in following the promptings of reason, not the dictates of power.[87] This objection raises large issues about practical reason that I am not able to address within the confines of this chapter. I will, however, make a few remarks aimed at dispelling the air of inconsistency.

The force of the objection depends on how we understand "rethinking within the terms of power." If it is interpreted to mean that we must accept existing gender norms and relations of power as circumscribing reflection, then the rethinking is, as the objection complains, disconnected from the deliberative interest. But "within the terms of power" should not be understood to imply such acceptance.[88] I take it to stand for the less controversial thesis that practical reflection must use as a point of departure norms (of gender, for example) and categories (of sexual orientation and conduct, for example), as well as images and desires, shaped by relations of power. Even in this interpretation of the phrase, however, the objection would still raise serious troubles *if* acknowledging the role of power-laden norms, categories, images, and desires in practical reflection required us to give up the idea that some patterns of conduct are better supported by reasons than others or the interest in pursuing those patterns. But no such nihilism about practical reason follows. Even if reflection uses power-laden norms and categories, we still have a reason to go to the store if we are hungry and know we can get food there; we still have a reason to believe that $2 + 2 = 4$, not to poison two-year-old children, and to be open to relevant evidence. To give such examples is not, of course, to answer the question: What is a reason (whether theoretical or practical)? That question lacks a simple answer. But whatever the correct explication, the intuitive force of claims about reasons of the kind just noted stands as an obstacle to any straightforward route from power-ladenness to nihilism.

A Digression on Method

I want to digress for a moment to comment on a feature of my argument that may not have gone unnoticed. I have principally cited women in

---

87. I am indebted to Susan Dwyer for raising this objection.

88. "[T]o operate within the matrix of power is not the same as to replicate uncritically relations of domination." Butler, *Gender Troubles*, 30. More generally, *Gender Trouble* is about displacing gender norms (148) by understanding identity generally and gender identities in particular as performances, grasping the diversity of those performances, and developing a vocabulary suited to that diversity (as distinct from the binary oppositions that dominate current discourse).

my discussion of the connections between pornography and the expressive and deliberative interests. There may be some temptation to dismiss their remarks as collaboration, yet further evidence that pornography constructs women as the "agents" of their own subordination—that all they "do" is collaborate. After all, "[i]t would be surprising if men eroticized dominance, practiced it, and enforced it over women, and there were no women who eroticized subordination. The surprise is that so many of us don't. . . ." [89] And there is a temptation as well to treat my citations of women as "hiding behind skirts."[90]

Both complaints have some force. But in the end I find it difficult simply to dismiss as collaboration considerations about the expressive and deliberative values of sexual expression. Those claims seem very plausible, and I see no *independent* evidence of collaboration.

As to hiding behind skirts: what else can I do to make the case for the expressive and deliberative interests? Refer to men who think pornography is great?[91]

Interests and Pornography, Redux

Let's return, then, to the interests and the regulations. Suppose one accepts the connections with expressive and deliberative interests and agrees about the importance of those interests. That may suffice to establish the first thesis I stated at the beginning of this section: that the same reasons that support stringent protections of, for example, artistic and political expression apply to expression that Indianapolis-style regulations would restrict. Still, the trouble for the regulations may not be obvious, for it might be thought that we now simply have a standoff. On the one hand, we have a case that pornography is seriously injurious; on the other, a case for connections with important human interests. Indeed, given the importance of substantive equality, appealing to the idea that it advances weighty interests will strike some as applauding rank self-indulgence or as worrying more about artists and male orgasms than about women's lives.

---

89. MacKinnon, "Does Sexuality Have a History?" 134; and MacKinnon, "On Collaboration," in *Feminism Unmodified*, 198–205.

90. I borrow the phrase from Catharine MacKinnon. She used it at the Brown conference mentioned at the beginning of these notes in connection with the phenomenon of citing women in arguments against pornography regulations.

91. But for some thoughtful remarks, see Kennedy, "Sexual Abuse," 210–11.

This objection misstates the argumentative situation. In my earlier discussion of the "Policy Case Against Regulation," I did not dismiss the conventional criticisms, but complained that they assume what needs showing—that the regulations must satisfy a very high burden of justification. The weight of the considerations in the lawyer's battery—about the speculativeness of arguments supporting regulation and the importance of exploring less restrictive alternatives for addressing abuse and subordination—is not freestanding; instead, it reflects the importance of the regulated target.[92] Thus, more speculative arguments will suffice when basic interests are not at stake. But given the importance of expressive and deliberative interests, and the connections between sexual expression and those interests, the high burden of justification is appropriate, and each of the four criticisms raises a serious objection to stringent regulations. Thus the second thesis: because the reasons for supporting stringent protections of, for example, artistic and political expression carry over to expression that Indianapolis-style regulations restrict, the lawyer's battery has some force; so we need to find other means to address the harms of subordination.

Alternative Strategies

Proposals to regulate pornography are animated by the damage pornography (allegedly) does to the cause of substantive sexual equality. I have criticized the remedies. But because substantive equality is a fundamental political value, critics need to say something about alternative remedies. What might some alternative strategies be for addressing the problems of subordination that pornography regulations aim to address? Here I want to make three suggestions.

Before getting to the suggestions, though, I emphasize that I offer them as supplements to, not substitutes for, familiar economic initiatives for achieving sexual equality and undermining the vulnerability that comes with inequality: say, policies of comparable worth to reduce unequal compensation within segregated labor markets, and a range of policies—including quality day care, flextime, parental leaves, mandatory support from absent fathers, equal legal entitlements to wage and salary income in the case of single-earner households, and a new frame-

---

92. This is the point of the familiar idea in constitutional law, that the level of scrutiny depends on the regulated target.

work of divorce law designed to equalize standards of living for post-divorce households—to address the unequal division of household labor.[93]

More immediately, then:

1. If the problem with pornography is that it legitimates sexual abuse and force by sexualizing it, then a first natural step would be to target sexual abuse—the abuse of women as women—more directly. Such targeting might, for example, include a tort of domestic sexual harassment modeled on workplace sexual harassment—including elements of quid pro quo and hostile environment harassment.[94] To be sure, the modeling would need to be very loose: sex is supposed to play some role in the lives of married couples; it is not supposed to play a role in the lives of people who happen to be working in the same office. But extreme sexual demands coupled with threats, or public sexual humiliation, might be forms of domestic sexual harassment. And such a tort could be a natural setting for actions against forcing pornography on a person, one element in the pornography ordinance I discussed earlier.

2. My second suggestion emerges from a claim commonly stated in debate about issues of expression: that the way to combat the injuries of speech is, as Justice Brandeis said, with more speech.[95] Brandeis's point is tirelessly repeated in discussions of freedom of expression. But the context of his remark is important. Brandeis was writing about a case of "subversive advocacy." He did not, however, address his remarks to the advocates: Anna Whitney, a 1920s leftist, was trying to speak; the state was shutting her up. Brandeis was reminding political elites of their vast resources for responding to arguments for revolutionary change: they might, for example, try to cure the social ills that prompt them or to argue the case against a revolutionary solution.

Addressed to less powerful groups, with restricted access to means of expression or whose voice is in other ways excluded or silenced, the easy injunction "More speech!" loses its force. Recommending "more speech" carries with it an obligation to ensure fair access to facilities of expression. It is unacceptable to impose a high burden on justifying restrictions on expression, justify that burden in part by the possibilities

---

93. See, for example, Okin, *Justice, Gender, and the Family,* chap. 8.

94. I take the proposal from Kennedy, "Sexual Abuse," 135.

95. *Whitney v. California.* This and subsequent paragraphs on fair access draw on Cohen, "Freedom of Expression."

of combating the harms of expression with more speech, and then not endorse the requirement of ensuring such facilities.

The implications of this observation in the area of conventional political speech are easy to see. In that setting, fair access means: ensuring open public forums for expression; affirming the importance of diverse broadcast messages and the role of fair access in contributing to such diversity; financing political campaigns through public resources; and regulating private political contributions and expenditures.

Applied to the case of subordination, the implications are less clear because the mechanisms of exclusion—or "silencing"—do not have principally to do with the distribution of material resources, but—it is argued—precisely with what is said. So here there may be serious tensions between a commitment to fair access and an opposition to regulating the content of expression.

But we should resist jumping too quickly to this conclusion, for other measures of empowerment that are more affirmative than regulations of expression may show real promise in combating silencing and exclusion. Among the possibilities are regular public hearings on sexual abuse—perhaps subsidies for women's organizations to hold such hearings[96]—or easier access of women to broadcast licenses. Moreover, insofar as silencing has economic foundations, efforts to ensure fair compensation and to address the traditional division of household labor would help.

3. Some regulations of violent pornography are not so vulnerable to the criticisms leveled earlier against the Indianapolis-style regulation. The central idea would be to define regulable pornography as a subcategory of the obscene expression that the Court now treats as having lower value. Consider an illustrative proposal.

Take obscenity, as currently understood. As I mentioned earlier, this category is defined so that material falls into it only if it is prurient, offensive, and lacking an intimate connection with First Amendment values. Putting to the side the puzzling role of prurience in the rationale for the category,[97] the idea is straightforward: low value reduces the case for protection and thereby permits regulation in the name of otherwise

---

96. For a more general discussion of associative approaches to reconciling egalitarian and liberal commitment, see Joshua Cohen and Joel Rogers, "Secondary Associations and Democratic Governance," *Politics and Society* 20, no. 4 (December 1992): 393—472.

97. If material is low-value and offensive, what does prurience add to the case for regulation?

insufficient concerns about offensiveness. Accepting for the sake of argument that obscenity does not have First Amendment protection, one natural strategy would be to regulate the subcategory of obscene materials that sexualize subordination or, more narrowly, that sexualize violence. The strong presumption against regulation would be reduced because none of the obscene has a strong claim to protection—that is how the category has been defined. Assuming that reduced presumption, it ought to be permissible to regulate obscenity where there is a case for harm—in particular, violent pornography.[98] Indeed, that case ought to carry some weight even if one rejects offensiveness altogether as a basis for regulation and so rejects obscenity regulations as currently understood.

If the principal reason for opposing Indianapolis-style pornography regulations is that the capacious category of the pornographic includes much that has substantial value, then a proposal along these lines may be workable. But the U.S. Supreme Court's decision in *R.A.V. v. St. Paul*—striking down a hate speech regulation—appears to block this subcategorization strategy.[99] In *R.A.V.*, the Court majority held that it was impermissible to target a regulation on the hate speech that falls into the regulable category of fighting words. According to the Court, it *is* permissible to target a regulation on all fighting words, or on the especially provocative fighting words, because the provocativeness of fighting words underlies the permission to regulate them. But it is not permissible to target the hateful or racially insulting subcategory of fighting words: that is, content regulation, as it would be content regulation to target violent pornography in which Republican men are the perpetrators.

By analogy, my guess is that the Court might accept regulations confined to obscene material that is grossly offensive—say, sex with animals or golden shower movies—for the offensiveness of obscenity is the reason for permitting its regulation. But they would not accept regulations targeted on the subcategory of obscene material that sexualizes violence: that would be content or viewpoint regulation. Here I disagree with Owen Fiss.[100] Fiss argues that regulations of pornographic obscenity would be acceptable because they would regulate the subset of

98. On the evidence that violent pornography is harmful, see Donnerstein, Linz, and Penrod, *Question of Pornography*.

99. R.A.V. v. St. Paul, 122 S. Ct. 2538 (1992).

100. See Fiss, "Freedom and Feminism," 2056, and 2056 n. 50.

obscene material that is especially extreme from the point of view of the very considerations that initially justify regulating obscenity: "to protect women from violence and sexual abuse."[101] But this seems wrong. The rationale for obscenity regulations lies in offensiveness, not in protecting women from violence and sexual abuse. For that reason, the court's position suggests a willingness to accept regulations of the grossly offensive, but not the pornographically obscene.

I think this is an indefensible position. And perhaps I am wrong about the Court's response to the subcategorization strategy in this area. But even if I am, I do not think that pressing for such regulations would be a very wise political investment; the third point in the lawyer's battery strikes me as relevant here. I doubt that regulations focused on sexually violent obscenity would do much work in addressing the harms of subordination. Suppose we agree that pornography, through cognitive or behavioral means, fuses sexual desire with the desire for subordination. Still, it seems highly implausible that such fusion occurs through the consumption of violent pornography, which is not especially prominent, even in outlets dedicated entirely to hard-core, sexually explicit magazines, videos, and paraphernalia.[102]

Here, however, we arrive at a familiar disagreement about effectiveness. It is not a disagreement of political principle—not a division on the importance of values of free expression and substantive equality—and treating it as one serves only to weaken support for those values.

Conclusion

Replying to a question put to her after a lecture several years ago, Catharine MacKinnon said that "equality is important but pleasure is too." And she criticized those who do not accept that "equality matters on any level approximate to pleasure."[103] The criticism is well taken.

---

101. Fiss, "Freedom and Feminism," 2056.
102. So it seems from outlets in Boston and New York, where sadomasochism (not always violent) is simply one among many niches—hetero, gay, bi, anal, oral, coeds, TV/TS, group, enema, and so on. More systematic surveys confirm the results of my causal inspection. For a discussion of some of the evidence on low and *declining* rates of violent imagery, see Lynn Segal's introduction to *Sex Exposed*, 6 (and the studies cited in notes 12 and 13).
103. MacKinnon, "Does Sexuality Have a History?" 134.

That's why we need to attack the injustice of inequality and subordination while accommodating the importance of pleasure. Perhaps there is no way to do both. But without a compelling case for its impossibility, such pessimism seems unwarranted.

Judicial Supremacy, the Concept of Law, and the Sanctity of Life

Frank I. Michelman

Government by Judiciary?

In the United States, where a written constitution and bill of rights have the force of law, we take for granted that judges of law will sometimes rule upon the legal validity of legislative and executive acts of government. The U.S. Constitution, as law, certainly outranks all other domestic legal material; that is the point of having the kind of constitution we have. It easily follows that when one party to a litigated dispute appeals to a governmental act in support of some legal claim or defense, the other party can always logically respond (and, as it happens, can also often plausibly respond) that the governmental act on which the first relies lacks legal force because it is against the Constitution. The court, then, in order to bring to some resolution the legal case before it—as required by the primary arbitral function for which courts are created—has somehow to dispose of a question of the legal validity of an act of government.[1]

It does not so easily follow, though, that judges ought ever or usually to decide such questions independently of the declared or evident views of responsible legislative bodies or other government officers. It's true that Americans have come to *expect* that judges will sometimes decide against the legal validity of statutes and other governmental acts,

---

This essay is a revised version of a lecture given at Amherst College during the 1993–94 academic year.

1. Needless to say, assertions of conflict between ordinary law and the Constitution are often fiercely contested because of disagreement over the relevant concrete meaning of the Constitution. The significance of this fact will occupy us very soon.

but this expectation is not logically compelled by putting together the higher-law status of constitutional material with the judge's responsibility to decide according to law the cases brought before her. A judgment of unconstitutionality of a statute, for example, always involves an *interpretation* of the arguably applicable constitutional-legal material, and judges could routinely treat as authoritative the supportive interpretations advanced, at least implicitly, by the presumedly law-abiding officials who enacted or who now seek to apply the law in question.[2] Now, the fact is that Americans have by and large come to count on judges for a much less deferential approach to constitutional interpretation. If our judiciaries did not stand ready to decide, on occasion, against the constitutionality of statutes, we would conclude that they were not doing their job. That job, thus understood, is what we call judicial review, and it is not easy to see how Americans could give it up without wrenching terribly out of shape our everyday legal culture and institutions as well as our more speculative theories of what constitutionalism, after all, is really about.

So we add the notion of an independent judiciary. Law judges are called independent when, by deliberate institutional arrangement—for example, having the judges chosen for lifetime service by a checks-and-balances procedure—their judgments in particular cases are sealed off from the communicated desires, preferences, and even considered legal judgments of other public officials and the citizenry at large.[3] Justices of the U.S. Supreme Court are independent in this sense, by express constitutional design.[4]

Judicial review, we have said, is an easy inference from combined commitments to higher-law constitutionalism and impartial adjudication of legal disputes, and judicial independence may seem a reasonable

---

2. To elaborate: If we presume the law-abiding motivations of those who enacted the law or who now invoke it, then by enacting or invoking it they have implicitly advanced an interpretation of the Constitution that would make their actions lawful. Quite conceivably, courts could have made it their general practice to follow, as authoritative, these constitutional interpretations implicitly advanced by presumedly law-abiding (and oath-abiding) legislative assemblies and executive officers.

3. Except, of course, insofar as the latter may be made argumentatively persuasive to the independent-minded judge. Judges may decide that they will, in some classes of cases or with respect to some classes of issues, defer to the judgments or directives of other governmental branches, but any such decisions to defer are themselves supposed to be arrived at by the judges independently, for what *they* have independently found to be good constitutional reasons.

4. See US Const, Art II, §2, cl. 2; Art III, §1.

sort of provision for bolstering the expectation of impartiality: that is, that legal outcomes are not affected by preferences unconstrained by motivation to decide in accordance with law. Now, the precise issue I consider here is neither judicial review nor judicial independence. Rather, it is the *finality* of authority over questions of constitutional-legal meaning that American practice grants to the judiciary, a finality that in kind and degree goes quite beyond what's required for the im-partial arbitral function of the law courts. The way things actually work in the American system, it's plain that when the Supreme Court declares unconstitutional a given type of government action, this event drasti-cally impairs the prospects of those, and there may be many, who not only favor action of that kind but believe it to be constitutionally cor-rect. Ronald Dworkin has recently stated the point with his accustomed éclat. "In practice," Dworkin writes, "politicians and people who hate a Supreme Court decision can only hope that new justices will [someday] be appointed who agree with them, and that . . . a revamped Supreme Court will overrule its own past decision. . . ."[5] Thus does Dworkin de-scribe a feature of American constitutional practice that we can distin-guish from judicial review *simpliciter* as "judicial supremacy"[6] or (some-what less amiably) "government by judiciary."[7]

---

5. Ronald Dworkin, *Life's Dominion: An Argument about Abortion, Euthanasia, and In-dividual Freedom* (New York: Knopf, 1993), 7. To which one might compare the (anticipa-tory) complaint of the anti-federalist essayist "Brutus":

[W]hen the power to [determine the sense of the constitution] is lodged in the hands of men independent of the people, and of their representatives, and who are not, constitutionally, accountable for their opinions, no way is left to controul them but *with a high hand and an outstretched arm*.

Brutus, "Essay XV," in *The Anti-federalist: Writings by the Opponents of the Constitution*, ed. Herbert J. Storing (Chicago: University of Chicago Press, 1985), 178, 187.

Dworkin, taking note of the possible recourses of constitutional amendment and im-peachment of judges, has called them "extremely difficult," "extreme," and "impractical" (*Life's Dominion*, 7, 145). "The main engines for disciplining judges," he has said, "are in-tellectual rather than political or legal" (145), and so he sees a good deal more room for ef-fective popular engagement in the processes of judicial nomination and confirmation. See Ronald Dworkin, "Mr. Liberty," *New York Review of Books* 41 (11 August 1994): 17, 22.

6. The term may have been coined by Charles G. Haines. See Haines, *The American Doctrine of Judicial Supremacy* (New York: MacMillan, 1914), quoted in Louis Boudin, *Gov-ernment By Judiciary* (New York: W. Godwin, 1932), 10. But see Brutus, "Essay XV," 186: "The judges are supreme—and no law, explanatory of the constitution, will be binding on them."

7. See Boudin, *Government by Judiciary*, 12. Boudin enclosed the term in quotation marks when he first introduced it, but he gave no source.

Now of course to give to this feature of our practice the name of "government by judiciary" is to assert, in effect, that when judges decide whether some questioned legislative or executive action comports with the Constitution, it is really *they*—the judges—who are doing the governing, not someone else speaking through them, not the authors and ratifiers of the Constitution who call themselves by the name of the People. In other words, the government-by-judiciary claim assumes that judicial decisions in these cases aren't mechanical, that judges doing this work are really *themselves deciding* major questions of political morality. That such is indeed the case is a view held by some staunch defenders of judicial supremacy, perhaps most prominently Ronald Dworkin. The gist of the view is that, for a combination of philosophical and empirical reasons, some of them pertaining to the pluralist character of modern liberal societies, the most important constitutional texts are and ought to be abstract[8] and, furthermore, that we can't regularly expect convergence on what the texts mean in various concrete applications.[9] Countless examples could be given. A suitable one for present purposes is disagreement over whether the Constitution's guarantee of "liberty" against unreasonable restriction by government extends to a woman's freedom to have a pregnancy aborted.

So legal questions of transgression by the government of constitutional limits and rights are and must be often reasonably disputable. It bears emphasizing that this statement may hold, for present purposes, regardless of anything that philosophers of language and knowledge or of morals and law may have to say about there being, in principle, a fact of the matter about the meaning of a prescriptive text such as the Constitution.[10] For present purposes, we can safely say—granting that such a statement may suggest to some that we don't know the meaning of "meaning"—that there being such a meaning-fact, if there is one, does not and cannot preclude frequent, persisting disagreement in practice over what that fact *is*, among contesting parties, all of whom must reasonably acknowledge that the others contest reasonably and in good faith.

---

8. John Rawls, for example, offers reasons why, in a normatively justifiable constitution serving a modern plural society, the important rights-conferring and power-limiting texts will have to be abstract. See John Rawls, *Political Liberalism* (New York: Columbia University Press, 1993).

9. For Dworkin's concurrence, see Dworkin, *Life's Dominion* 145.

10. See, for example, Ronald Dworkin, *Taking Rights Seriously* (Cambridge: Harvard University Press, 1977), 81–130.

A leading expositor of this view in the United States, Ronald Dworkin, expounds it eloquently in *Life's Dominion*.[11] One of Dworkin's aims in that book is to defend the Supreme Court's repeated decisions that a woman's freedom to have a pregnancy aborted receives protection from the Constitution's general guarantees of "liberty" against arbitrary or excessive government restriction.[12] A major claim in Dworkin's defense is that these decisions properly treat the Constitution as "a statement of abstract moral ideals" that "each generation must reinterpret for itself."[13] There are, Dworkin says, no "mechanical" rules to be extracted from the fund of "majestic abstractions" in the Bill of Rights. Those who seek "genuine" constraint on government can find it in the Constitution, but only interpretatively, through an activity of "argument" in which participants do their collective best "to construct, reinspect, and revise, generation by generation, the skeleton of freedom and equality of concern that [the Constitution's] great clauses, in their majestic abstraction, command."[14]

We must, Dworkin goes on to say, accept that, in this effort, honest participants are bound to disagree about "dozens" of "inescapable . . . moral issues."[15] So far, at least, as Dworkin is concerned, the reason for this—to repeat—isn't that there are no facts of the matter about constitutional-legal meanings. Dworkin is someone who has famously maintained that there are such facts. He has maintained that in every dispute over the concrete legal meanings of our constitutional clauses guaranteeing "liberty" and "equal protection of the laws," one of the contending parties is as a matter of fact right and the other wrong.[16] It follows that the deciders—the judges—are obligated to decide in accord with the "actual" meanings of the clauses. Their charge is to act as the clauses "in fact" require, which in Dworkin's view means deciding in accordance with "the best, most accurate understanding of liberty and equal citizenship" in the concrete circumstances of the case and the times. Now of course it's clear that what this most accurate understanding (granting such a thing's existence) *is* is a matter distinct from what the

---

11. Dworkin, *Life's Dominion*.
12. See US Const, Amends V, XIV.
13. Dworkin, *Life's Dominion*, 26, 111.
14. Ibid., 145.
15. Ibid.
16. See Dworkin, *Taking Rights Seriously*; Dworkin, *A Matter of Principle* (Cambridge: Harvard University Press, 1985), 119–45; Dworkin, *Law's Empire* (Cambridge: Harvard University Press, Belknap Press, 1986), 76–86.

decider "thinks" it to be. Yet it's equally clear, as Dworkin says, that a decider has, in practice, no way to carry out her charge except by "acting on [her] own convictions" of what is (in fact) required.[17]

The upshot, in Dworkin's words, is that, "for all practical purposes,"

> the federal courts, and finally the Supreme Court, have the last word about what rights the Constitution affirms and protects, and what the national and state governments therefore cannot do. So some of the most important political decisions that any community must make . . . have been decided for Americans by judges, rather than by elected representatives of the people.[18]

There you have the clearest possible statement of the sense in which the American system of government is, in part, one of government by judiciary.

It is true that Dworkin's account of these matters is disputed. Some think that constitutional interpretation can and ought to be mechanical. Others depreciate the Supreme Court's role in American politics by envisioning the Court as sooner or later controlled by popular wishes and views—as ultimately armed with no more than a suspensive veto. But what I specifically want to explore here is defense of the Supreme Court's role by theorists like Dworkin who do staunchly defend the role even while describing the Court as a holder of something that approaches final authority over fairly contestable political moral issues of the greatest interest to the country. The position that concerns us here is the one that says: "We do have a significant lot of government by an independent judiciary and it's quite okay that we do."

Why be concerned about this position? For starters, let us just say because of the banal reason for objection, at least prima facie, to government by judiciary. If the high court has such a decisive role as Dworkin says in resolving for the country major debatable questions of the constitutional fundamentals, why should we not say of the American practice that it concedes to high court judges extra-large helpings of political franchise? It is not immediately obvious how to square equality of concern and respect in politics with denial of opportunity to everyone to have their judgments counted fairly along with the judgments of

---

17. Dworkin, *Life's Dominion*, 137.
18. Ibid., 120.

others, when it is the case that the practical import of the country's fundamental laws undergoes significant redetermination by persons casting judgments on the question.[19] In Dworkin's view (which I fully share) of constitutional interpretation, that would seem to be precisely what goes on when voting majorities of high court judges resolve contested issues of constitutional-legal meaning. Why, then, do not Dworkin and I and other devotees of political equality make it our business to call judicial supremacy into question, actively and persistently—by, for example, working hard at the development of practicable institutional alternatives?

Judicial Leadership without Judicial Finality?

It is best, for present purposes, to pose this question in a way that isolates as far as possible the question of judicial *leadership* in the field of constitutional interpretation from that of the (relative) *finality* of judicial action in this field. Judicial leadership, I want to stipulate, makes a clear kind of sense. Constitutional interpretation is challenging work. Whether there is such a thing as getting it right, there is doubtless such a thing as doing it well, and prudence would suggest that we have strong reasons, other things being equal, for contriving to have it done as well as can be managed. Granted, people disagree sharply over what it *is* to do this work well. Here, however, where we want to concede as much as we fairly can to the case for judicial supremacy, we do best to assume strong advantages accruing to the work from well-honed dialectical and judgmental capabilities; from a cultivated sense of the distinction between public and personal reason;[20] and from a live and broad working knowledge of the law, along with a studied grasp of the country's deep political-moral culture.[21]

In sum, we stipulate that legal-interpretative work benefits strongly from inputs of learning, skill, experience, and esprit—capacities that grow under professional training and nurture and that, therefore, we can reasonably hope to find in special concentration among occupants of a judicial office that itself (as we further obligingly assume)

---

19. See Frank I. Michelman, "On Regulating Practices With Theories Drawn From Them," in *Theory and Practice (Nomos XXXVII)*, ed. Ian Shapiro and Judith Wagner DeCew (New York: New York University Press, 1994), 327–30.

20. See Rawls, *Political Liberalism*, lecture 6.

21. See Dworkin, *Law's Empire*, 227.

has been staffed in good faith. Correlatively, we assume—all of this *arguendo*—that the preponderance of nonjudicial citizens are, by average capacity and life experience, less well situated to succeed in the work of constitutional-legal interpretation. We assume they stand in need of support from judges and others schooled to the work, who can lay before them the relevant legal and other information, including various lines of argument already known to be available, and induct them into the spirit of the task.

Here, now, is what we do *not* assume. For reasons that will appear, we do not assume that, under the conditions of judicial leadership just stated, ordinary citizens and their electorally accountable representatives are intellectually or motivationally incapable of arguing competently or judging honestly among contestant constitutional-legal interpretations or of deciding on what occasions to take constitutional interpretation into their own hands. Our arguendo assumption is that the people at large are well served by judicial interpretative leadership. That is not the same thing as being finally governed by judges.

Are judicial leadership and judicial finality, however, workably severable in practice? Is there some way to excise judicial finality, but not leadership, from an institutional system that remains committed to ideas of (1) impartial dispute resolution according to law and (2) a constitution as paramount law that all officials, judges included, are obliged to recognize and honor insofar as it has application to the matters officially before them? It is not difficult to conceive in theory of such an excision. Here is one way of doing it that can serve as a thought experiment for us: We could amend the Constitution to authorize some body composed of specially elected representatives of the people (a Council of Revision, let's call it) to reconsider on its own motion the Supreme Court's concrete interpretations of constitutional meanings and (when so resolved) to issue mandates contradicting those interpretations that would thenceforth be binding on the courts. Such a reform would leave undisturbed the judicial function of resolving social disputes in accordance with the standing law as it may be given to the judges to understand that law. Moreover, a body thus empowered to speak to questions of constitutional meaning only after the Supreme Court had spoken to contrary effect would always carry the onus of contradicting the Court, and so such a scheme could preserve for the country—in whatever degree the country chose—the benefits of trained, specialized, and experienced judicial leadership in the field of constitutional-legal interpretation.

No doubt it would be a challenging task to draft and put into operation such a reform so as to make it workable and fair. There is, however, no a priori reason to think the venture impossible, and anyway my point in posing the thought experiment is my expectation that the overwhelming majority of judicial supremacy's supporters will recoil sharply from the very aim of materially increasing the frequency with which electorally accountable agents would displace the Supreme Court as the final arbiter of constitutional-legal meaning. My question is: Why is that? Why are we so attached to government by independent judiciary (those of us who are)?

Law, Principle, and Government by Judiciary

There is an obvious possible answer to this question, one that's often elided or obscured in the justificatory arguments that academic theorists propose for judicial supremacy, and I want before going further to put this obvious possible answer squarely on the table. This obvious possible answer is: We favor government by independent judiciary just because of fear of the consequences of the conceivable alternatives. I mean specifically the consequences as gauged by the goodness of the laws and of the government of the country. I mean a fear that replacing the independent judiciary, as last-word constitutional interpreter, with the people's tribunes would result in giving the country worse government than we get now, maybe much worse. Such a fear seems by no means crazy.

Crazy or not, though, it is embarrassing for Abraham Lincoln's posterity to deny that government of the people by the people can safely be risked where it would seem to many to count most, that is, at the point of giving contemporaneous concrete meaning to the fundamental laws of the country. Perhaps in part for that reason, we Americans are accustomed to hearing judicial supremacy defended on loftier-sounding grounds than plain prudential fear of the consequences of giving it up. One of these loftier lines of defense is, broadly put, that government by judiciary simply flows from the idea of *law* contained in the liberal constitutional ideal of government under law.

In *Life's Dominion*,[22] Ronald Dworkin writes as if judicial supremacy is an obviously fitting accompaniment—indeed a foregone im-

---

22. As I point out subsequently, Dworkin has elsewhere offered more guarded views.

plication—of another idea he says we ought to approve: that is, the idea that constitutional law is best conceived as consisting in principle and as being principled. His message is that this idea of the principled character and substance of constitutional law is itself so compelling that we do best to accept the judicial-supremacy baggage that comes along with it, despite any objection we might otherwise have to the baggage.

Dworkin contends against adversaries who hold that our Supreme Court's abortion-rights decisions must be wrong because the enactors of the broad constitutional guarantees of liberty and equality on which the decisions rely had no intention of affecting in any way the government's powers to prevent abortion. This kind of objection, Dworkin says, makes a sadly wrong choice between two ways of reading the Constitution. It chooses to construct what Dworkin calls a "constitution of *detail*"—a "limited list of the particular individual rights that statesmen now dead thought important" (a list "unlikely to have great unity or even consistency"). Dworkin's preferred alternative, we've already seen, is to construct a "constitution of *principle*" that lays down "abstract ideals of political morality that each generation of citizens, lawyers, and judges must together explore and reinterpret," when and as it becomes necessary "to decide what these standards mean in concrete circumstances."[23]

Dworkin notices a certain apparent difficulty attending his position. Take, for example, the question of whether the Constitution's guarantees of "liberty" and "equality" mean to restrict the government's powers to prohibit abortions. It follows from the idea of a constitution of principle, Dworkin says (but without explaining how it does), that it is the justices of the Supreme Court who will "have to" decide for the country this question of constitutional meaning.[24] That, he says, the justices can do only by answering, on the country's behalf, "intractable,

---

23. Dworkin, *Life's Dominion*, 26, 119. In view of Dworkin's perception of the American judicial review practice as one of strong judicial supremacy, his reference at 26 to reinterpretation by "citizens" along with "lawyers and judges" seems somewhat loose. (See also Frank I. Michelman, "Foreword: Traces of Self-Government," *Harvard Law Review* 100 (1986): 4, 66–73.) That formulation should be compared with the statement at 119 of *Life's Dominion* that a constitution of principle "leaves it to statesmen and judges to decide what these standards mean in concrete circumstances."

24. Dworkin, *Life's Dominion*, 120. Dworkin here agrees with the view of the three-justice plurality opinion in Planned Parenthood v. Casey, 112 S. Ct. 2791, 2816 (1992), where the plurality portrayed the American people as bound by their aspiration to a rule of law to grant the Court "authority to decide their constitutional cases and speak before all others for their ideals." See Dworkin, *Life's Dominion*, 126.

profound questions of political morality that philosophers, statesmen, and citizens have debated for many centuries with no prospect of agreement." The upshot is that the rest of the country must abide by "the deliverances of a majority of the justices"—whose "insight into these great issues," Dworkin disarmingly writes, "does not seem spectacularly special."[25]

As we've already seen, Dworkin readily agrees that this arrangement gives strikingly great powers to independent judges. Recall his summation: "Some of the most important political decisions that any community must make" are "decided for Americans by judges." As Dworkin further allows, many Americans find it objectionable that the judges should have this kind of power. But Dworkin considers "misplaced" this public "suspicion" of partial government by judiciary, a practice that he suggests just rides along with the ideal of government under law as principle.[26]

Dworkin does not spell out the tie between judicial finality and law as principle. What is it, precisely? There is, perhaps, a temptation to think (I don't say Dworkin thinks this, or argues it) that constitutional review by the tribunes of the people would war conceptually with the very idea of a principled constitutional law and the very point of conceiving that we have such a law. The thought might be unpacked this way: If, in a representative democracy, the people grant themselves or their representatives authority to interpret by their own lights the law of the Constitution, then it is idle to speak any longer of government limited by law. Because what is it, after all, that makes a limit on government a legal limit, if not entrenchment against the beck and call of the governors—meaning, in a representative democracy, the people and their representatives—to alter or relax it? But this conceptual argument evaporates on closer inspection. Giving the people or their elected representatives (in contradistinction to independent judges) the last word on questions of concrete constitutional-legal meaning does not *conceptually* defeat either the point of constitutional-legal entrenchment or the principled character of law. The proof is easy.

We start again from the observation that concrete applications of constitutional law are often subject to reasonable dispute. We then imagine the people, acting through representative institutions, addressing

---

25. Dworkin, *Life's Dominion*, 120.
26. To be precise, Dworkin writes of "public suspicion of judges having the power that the principled view [of the Constitution] assigns them" (*Life's Dominion*, 123).

such disputes and doing so in good faith, just as we are pleased to imagine judges addressing them—that is, addressing them as questions both of principle and of the meaning of the law that is. Assuming the people do thus vote their good-faith judgments of true, principled legal meaning, a popularly based procedure for resolving constitutional-legal interpretative questions no more contradicts the idea of law as principled constraint than does allowing such questions to be resolved by the votes of shifting majorities of high court judges.

Under government by judiciary, we are pleased to believe that constitutional-legal entrenchments do significantly *exist*. But obviously the condition of our believing this is our further attribution to the judges of a striving in good faith to decide constitutional-legal questions objectively, by exercises of a special form of what John Rawls in his recent book calls public reason.[27] If we made a like attribution to the people and their electorally accountable representatives when called upon to decide such questions, then constitutional-legal entrenchments would likewise exist under a system of popularly based constitutional interpretation. There is certainly nothing in the concept of law that requires us to make such attributions of objectivity to an independent judiciary but forbids us making them to electorally accountable representatives. So it is not true that the idea of government under law already conceptually contains the idea of government by judiciary or already conceptually rules out provision for popularly based determinations of concrete constitutional-legal meaning.

Nor, it should now be clear, can the trouble with government by judiciary be dispelled by establishing a congruence between higher-law constitutionalism and democracy. In *Life's Dominion*, Dworkin calls it a "precondition of legitimate democracy" that "government is required to treat individual citizens as equals, and to respect their fundamental liberties and dignity," including most especially their liberties of conscience.[28] If government fails in that obligation, Dworkin says, there is no "genuine democracy" because in that event "the majority has no le-

---

27. See Rawls, *Political Liberalism*, lecture 6.
28. "Because we cherish dignity, we . . . place the right of conscience at [freedom's] center, so that a government that denies the right is totalitarian. . . . Because we honor dignity, we demand democracy, and we define it so that a constitution that permits a majority to deny freedom of conscience is democracy's enemy. . . . Whatever view we take about abortion, . . . we want the right to decide for ourselves, and we should therefore be ready to insist that any honorable constitution, any genuine constitution of principle, will guarantee that right for everyone." Dworkin, *Life's Dominion*, 239.

gitimate title to govern."[29] But it seems plain that these remarks, true as they might be, do not make a reason for accepting government by judiciary. To proclaim the illegitimacy of government unconstrained by a higher law of equality, dignity, and liberty is surely to affirm that these preconditions of legitimacy—equality, dignity, and liberty—can no more be matters of fixed and certain constitutional "detail" than any other fundamentals of political morality entrenched as constitutional law. (Think, for example, of current controversies over the constitutional implications of political campaign finance regulation and race-conscious legislative districting.) They are—they must be, on Dworkin's line of thought—cast and construed as demands of principle, abstractions whose concrete meaning lies waiting in the bosom of expectant interpretation, in historical setting, by and for the generations in their turns.

Each event of interpretation may pose, as before, one or more of those "intractable, profound questions of political morality that philosophers, statesmen, and citizens have debated for centuries with no prospect of agreement." And so the question remains, as before, why independent judges, rather than the people and their engaged representatives, should hold the ultimate interpretative authority. Positing that the legitimacy of government rides on getting the answers right may add urgency and poignancy to the choice. It may heighten our sense of danger and risk. But it does not otherwise alter the terms on which we choose. Independent judges surely can fail; an engaged people, as we are for the moment supposing, can possibly succeed; neither can do better than their best. The choice remains what it is: Shall it be the people to whom it is given to live the people's lives or, to speak more precisely, that aspect of their lives consisting of the exercise of responsibility for the morally charged meanings of the fundamental laws of their country, or shall it be a small handful of guardedly independent judges "whose insight into these great issues does not seem spectacularly special"? Justice Robert Jackson, a realist, unforgettably wrote: "We [justices of the Supreme Court] are not final because we are infallible but we are infallible because we are final."[30] The question remains to be answered: What good reason have Americans to grant finality to the fallible? Why ought they to create the fallible as infallible?

29. Ibid., 123.
30. Brown v. Allen, 344 U.S. 443, 532, 540 (1953) (Jackson, J., concurring in the result).

I have already mentioned that Dworkin deprecates public "suspicion" of government by judiciary. Of Americans who harbor this suspicion, *Life's Dominion* speaks, I think, in accents of disparagement. The book presents these Americans as men and women of little faith who prefer certainty and "safety" to the challenge and "danger" of life in the open with a constitution of principle.[31] Disliking to submit to judicial interpretative authority, these Americans seek refuge (ignobly, one gets the sense) in a constitution of detail. It's not necessarily that they can't see the value of what is lost by thus constructing the Constitution as "a collection of detailed separate and independent rules put together like a postage stamp collection from different parts of American history."[32] It's just that they'd rather treat the Constitution in this shameful way than submit to rule by the justices.

But this reading of the case seems unearned, gratuitous. Among Americans concerned that we grant judges too much power, there may be many who would agree wholeheartedly that our Constitution is best treated as one of principle constantly demanding interpretation. Dworkin's argument in *Life's Dominion* rhetorically poses the choice we face as one between accepting government by judiciary and forsaking the ideal of the constraint of government by limits that are both institutionally effective and morally principled. Unremarked there is the fact that government by judiciary is not required—at least not conceptually—by the idea of legal constraint of governors by a definite set of abstract political-moral principles.

Now to restate what I've just been saying: Dworkin persuasively asserts the moral superiority of the "principled" over the "detailed" view of the Constitution. "[U]nderstood as one of principle," he writes, our Constitution "provides a better form of government than any in which the legislative and executive branches of government are legally free to disregard fundamental principles of justice and decency."[33] What's now at issue, though, is not this better-form-of-government claim. What's under consideration here is what (if anything) follows regarding government by judiciary. In *Life's Dominion*, Dworkin's rhetoric presupposes that the ideal of government under law as principle gives Americans obvious reason to accept government by judiciary.

Elsewhere, addressing directly the question of the ideal's implications for judicial supremacy, Dworkin has offered the more circumspect

---

31. See Dworkin, *Life's Dominion*, 122.
32. Ibid.
33. Ibid., 123.

view that while the law-as-principle ideal leaves theoretically open the choice for or against government by judiciary, Americans have very reasonably resolved this choice, as a matter of historical fact, in the affirmative.[34] Always, though, he defends this arrangement as entirely benign and comfortably at home with constitutional values of liberty, equality, and democracy. We have confirmed that institutional arrangements for judicial supremacy do not follow *conceptually* from ideals of democracy and government under law as principle. Later on we'll briefly consider how these ideals might *instrumentally* recommend such arrangements. But to set the stage for that, I now want to suggest that Dworkin himself has provided, in *Life's Dominion*, strong grounds for wanting to resist the idea that government by judiciary follows *at all* from ideas of democracy and government under law as principle. For according to Dworkin's own central argument in that book, it seems that government by judiciary comes at a high cost in human dignity and the intrinsic value (or what Dworkin also calls the "sanctity") of human life.

The Sanctity of Life

In *Life's Dominion*, Dworkin offers guidance on a number of constitutional-legal controversies, including controversy over abortion rights. What binds these discussions together is that they all draw on various facets and implications of an interpretative account that Dworkin proposes for the strongly held inclination (which Dworkin sees as widely shared across society) to attach what he calls "intrinsic" value to human life. When Dworkin speaks of our valuing human life intrinsically, he means we recognize this value not just as an aspect of the interests of individuals, in deference to claims of right issuing from individuals in virtue of their interests in their own lives, but rather as a freestanding value just in itself.[35] An evident main concern of the book is to clarify

---

34. See Dworkin, *Law's Empire*, 355–57. Carefully read with reference to distinctions I have drawn earlier, the argument in the cited pages expressly addresses only the question of judicial *review*, about which I raise no question, and not that of (relative) judicial *finality* with which I am here concerned. In a later (but as this book goes to press, still unpublished) writing, Dworkin offered a similar observation in a context apparently covering the finality question, too. See Ronald Dworkin, "The Moral Reading and the Majoritarian Default" (paper presented to New York University Colloquium on Constitutional Theory, New York, 16 March 1995), 24–26.

35. It's not, Dworkin insists, that we can or do value human life only because or insofar as some rights-bearing creature claims it. See Dworkin, *Life's Dominion* 11, 71–72. But one must also note that Dworkin's elaborated account of this value makes the *sources* of it, the grounds of our recognition of it, essentially include perceptions of individuality and

the bearing of our appreciation of life's intrinsic value on the proper disposition of various kinds of individual-rights claims that can be perceived to engage in one way or another a concern for this value.

Dworkin attributes to us, his audience, as inhabitants of Western
political culture, a particular conception of human-life value.[36] What,
ultimately, we revere in human life, Dworkin suggests, is its manifestation of creativity. We value human life intrinsically insomuch as we see
this life "as *lived*, as made up of the actions, decisions, motives and
events that compose what we . . . call a biography."[37] For us, one basic
source of human life's intrinsic value lies in appreciation of the fact of
the human individual's capacity for self-creation.[38] True, individual
self-creation is not the only kind of manifest creativity that, according to
Dworkin, inspires our reverence for human life. It is, however, an essential and indispensable source of that reverence. Human life is also a
manifestation of creative forces attributed to God or nature and to society. We can read Dworkin as saying that it's our perception of the con-
fluence of all these creativities in the life story of each individual that
gives rise to our sense of the sanctity of life as each person lives it.[39]

This rooting of our sense of life's sanctity in self-creative capacity,
Dworkin urges, helps explain something that is obvious and important,
but otherwise puzzling, about how we judge the values of lives. It is a
fact, he says, that people recognize themselves and others as having
what he calls "critical" as well as "experiential" interests. My critical interests are the concerns I have about the conduct of my life as I shape
and live it over its entire span. They are the concerns I have about what

---

self-creativity. What we value, according to Dworkin, is not free-floating élan vital but life
as lived, life as distributed to individuals and manifested in their life stories. Only thus is
Dworkin able to argue *from* the intrinsic value of human life, *through* notions of critical and
dignitary interests attributed to individuals, *to* propositions of individual autonomy
rights. For the suggestion that Dworkin's commitment ab initio to arguments of this kind
may undermine his initial characterization of the value of human life as detached from
the recognitional claims of individuals, see T. M. Scanlon, "Partisan for Life," *New York Review of Books* 40 (15 July 1993), 45, 49–50.

36. Dworkin, *Life's Dominion*, 166.

37. Ibid., 83.

38. My notion of "source" here follows that of Judith Jarvis Thomson. See Thomson,
The Realm of Rights (Cambridge: Harvard University Press 1990), 31–33, 212. Thomson in-
quires into the sources of our having individual (moral) rights, meaning by "source" a
supportive consideration that is not itself already a moral judgment. A moral judgment
such as the judgment that individuals have rights must ultimately, Thomson says, reach
down to sources that "consist in some feature of us."

39. See Dworkin, *Life's Dominion*, 76–77.

courses of action, from among those from time to time open to me, will
in fact contribute toward making my life *as mine* a good or successful as
distinguished from a wasted life. My critical interests thus reflect my
"critical judgments" rather than just my "experiential preferences."
They are my interests in wanting what I ought to want for the sake of
the value of my life as I am about creating it.[40]

Dworkin treats as a given fact that most people recognize both that
we have critical interests and that these are, indeed, the most important
interests we have. For this fact he seeks an explanation, meaning an account of it "from the inside" that will enable us to "understand intro-
spectively how [critical interests] connect with other large beliefs we
have about life and death and why human life has intrinsic value."[41]
Not surprisingly, Dworkin locates the source of our having critical interests just where he found the source of our sense of the sanctity of life,
that is, in the perceived fact of human self-creative capacity.[42] Critical
interests, he says, refer to a regulative idea that lies "at the very foundation of our ethical lives," the idea of personal integrity.[43] Thus, at the
core of life's intrinsic value for us lies, by Dworkin's account, the challenge of integrity, the challenge of living our life whole.

By now we have before us the makings of an explanation—still
rooted where our sense of life's sanctity is said to be, in self-creative
capacity—for the importance that liberals attach to human moral rights
of personal autonomy. Such rights, says Dworkin, "make self-creation
possible." They protect "the capacity to express one's own character . . .
in the life one leads." Autonomy rights enable each of us "to be responsible for shaping our lives according to our own . . . personality" so that
we can each "be . . . what we have made of ourselves," insofar as—the
qualification bears noting—"a scheme of rights can make this possi-

40. Ibid., 200–202, 215.
41. Ibid., 204.
42. "Someone's convictions about his own critical interests are opinions about what
it means for his *own* life to go well, and these convictions can therefore best be understood
as a special application of his general commitment to the sanctity of life. He . . . treats his
. . . life as something sacred for which *he* is responsible, something *he* must not waste. He
thinks it intrinsically important that he live well, and with integrity." Ibid., 215–16.
43. Ibid., 205–6. For fuller development of the claim that the challenge of integrity
lies at the core of life's value for us, see Ronald Dworkin, *Foundations of Liberal Equality*,
vol. 11, Tanner Lectures on Human Values (Salt Like City: University of Utah, 1990). For
doubts about the universality of appeal of Dworkin's argument from the ideal of integrity
to constitutional-legal autonomy rights, see Patrick Neal, "Dworkin on The Foundations
of Liberal Equality," *Legal Theory* 1 (1995): 205, 219–24.

ble."[44] In this account, the intermediary term between integrity (or critical interest) and autonomy rights is *responsibility:* Autonomy is or ought to be a right (against the government) because and insofar as it allows for the sort of responsibility involved in meeting the challenge of integrity.

The idea of the value of moral responsibility, as thus developed, carries a heavy load in Dworkin's defense of the abortion decisions. Suppose we find a political community united on the goal of maintaining among its members a devotion to the intrinsic value of human life. At the same time, though, we find the members sharply divided over whether particular decisions to abort pregnancies positively serve and express this value or rather disserve and insult it.[45] Then, Dworkin says, we need to decide whether, in these circumstances, the community's proper aim is one of "conformity" or "responsibility." Is it that "citizens obey rules and practices that the majority believes best express and protect the sanctity of life," or is it that "citizens recognize that fundamental intrinsic values are at stake in [abortion] decisions and decide reflectively, . . . out of examined conviction," thus developing "their own sense of when and why life is sacred?" If responsibility is the aim, then "we must leave citizens free . . . to decide as they think right, because that is what moral responsibility entails."[46]

Now plainly the strength of Dworkin's argument in favor of responsibility over conformity depends on his proposition that an indispensable source, for us, of human life's intrinsic value is the human capacity to steer by the star of critical interest. For it's by the force of that proposition that the community cannot well vindicate its commitment to human life's intrinsic value, in the context of procreational decision, by any means that subordinates responsibility to conformity. To elaborate: When the community's aim is that people's concrete procreative decisions and corresponding actions should serve and express the community's shared regard for the intrinsic value of human life; when the moral question of the consonance of particular procreative decisions with the community's pro life aim is itself a matter that is deeply and sincerely contested within the community; and when, at the same time, *what makes human life intrinsically valuable is the capacity of human indi-*

---

44. Dworkin, *Life's Dominion,* 224.
45. Dworkin's argument here takes it as established that an early fetus is not a person endowed with its own *right* to life. See, for example, *Life's Dominion,* 169–70.
46. Ibid., 151–52.

viduals to take responsibility for shaping critically valuable lives for themselves; then—surely this is Dworkin's point—the community cannot coherently express or pursue its commitment to human life's intrinsic value by subordinating responsibility to conformity, because in these circumstances of deep moral disagreement, to block responsibility is to block the capacity for critical self-direction and thereby defeat intrinsic value. In the process, moreover, rights are sacrificed. For, in Dworkin's view, from our culture's rooting of human life's intrinsic value in people's capacities for critical self-direction grows our culture's conception of moral dignity: "that people have the moral right—and the moral responsibility—to confront the most fundamental questions about the meaning and value of their own lives for themselves, answering to their own consciences and convictions."[47]

So subordinating responsibility to conformity would, in these circumstances, exact a heavy immediate toll of both intrinsic value and human moral rights. And Dworkin claims it would further have a longer-term deleterious effect. (Just here is where the tension becomes most apparently acute between Dworkin's specific defense of the Supreme Court's abortion-rights cases and his general support of government by judiciary.) Dworkin asks rhetorically:

> Does a state protect a contestable value best by encouraging people to accept it *as* contestable, understanding that they are responsible for deciding for themselves what it means? Or does the state protect a contestable value best by itself deciding, through the political process, which interpretation is the right one, and then forcing everyone to conform?[48]

This question echoes the protest of generations of critics of American government by judiciary.[49] One can hardly help asking: Why is Dworkin's rhetorical question not equally strongly applicable to the contested *political* values of equality and liberty as found in the American constitution of principle, when the concrete meanings of these val-

---

47. Ibid., 166.
48. Ibid., 151.
49. See, for example, James Bradley Thayer, *John Marshall* (Boston: Houghton Mifflin, 1901), 103; Learned Hand, "The Contribution of an Independent Judiciary to Civilization," in *The Spirit of Liberty: Papers and Addresses*, ed. Irving Dilliard (New York: Knopf, 1960), 155, 164; Robin West, "Progressive and Conservative Constitutionalism," *Michigan Law Review* 88 (1990): 641, 713–21.

ues are called into question by disputes over the constitutionality (and the political morality) of government curbs on abortion? Do we protect these contested political-moral values—liberty and equality—better by laying on the people at large their own responsibility for interpretative judgment of their application to the abortion question or by inviting the people to conform to the directives of a Supreme Court majority? Why, indeed, is the same question not equally applicable to every contested political-moral issue of how best to protect the abstract values of freedom and equality whose concrete meanings can only be found, from generation to generation, through constitutional interpretation? The burning question for us is whether all of Dworkin's intrinsic-value and right-based arguments against subordinating responsibility to conformity don't hold as forcefully for the morally charged and deeply contestable issues raised for the generations by their needs to interpret the grand abstractions of the constitution of principle in order to make them concretely trenchant. For it seems plain that much intrinsic value is lost (assuming this is what government by judiciary does) by cutting off the mass of the people from responsible engagement with the processes of judgment that pour concrete meaning into the basic laws of their country.

To the argument I am offering here, there is an important objection waiting to be raised. The objection is that, unlike procreational decisions, which (at least as Dworkin conceives them) are practically distributable to individuals in a way such that no one need be bound by anyone else's decision, constitutional-legal interpretation is an activity that's indissolubly social or collective.[50] What is interpretatively decided for the legal case of one must be binding for the like legal cases of all; that much is indeed already conceptually contained in the idea of government under law. Unlike the decision whether or not to have an abortion, the decision whether or not to subject such decisions to legal

---

50. Some would stoutly deny that the alleged difference exists. No man or woman, (or preborn) is an island, they would say; the bell tolls for us all when it tolls for any one, and everyone's world is affected by anyone's decision to terminate human (fetal) life. Dworkin would perhaps respond that for the state to restrict liberty on such a communitarian-moral ground would be for it to violate the liberal principle of resource-equality by giving political weight to external preferences. See, for example, Dworkin, *Foundations of Liberal Equality*, 37–38, 116–17 (1990). Later in this chapter, we'll glance briefly at whether adequate protection of this asserted basic liberal principle requires government by judiciary. We'll grant Dworkin there, as we do here, his substantive claim that external moral disapprobation cannot by itself justify coercive restraint of liberty.

restriction is not a "matter of individual conduct" that those who speak for the state can possibly leave up to someone else.[51] And in the case of such indissolubly social decisions, it may be said, since there is no possible escape from subordination of responsibility to conformity, then there is no point, either, in bewailing frustration of responsibility. (Dworkin, remember, calls for constitutional arrangements and understandings that "allow ... us to ... be, *to the extent a scheme of rights can make this possible,* what we have made of ourselves.")

But still it seems that to conclude thus is to give up on responsibility too soon. It is true, of course, that a constitutional-interpretative decision for or against procreative autonomy is indissolubly social insofar as we assume that the decision must bind (while it lasts) every inhabitant of the country. But the fact that conformity is thus unavoidable does nothing, in itself, to detract from the value of responsibility. It does nothing to wipe away the loss of responsibility and intrinsic value that might have been realized under arrangements that would call on citizens, both severally and collectively, to take responsibility—not just *in foro interno* or speculatively at the dinner table but socially, actively, practically—for their own judgments on various profound moral questions, as Dworkin correctly calls them, of the concrete meanings of their country's basic laws, such as the question of whether the Constitution is rightly construed to shield abortion choices from prohibition by government.

Engagement and Accuracy

Engagement

It is both feasible and right to bring questions of legal content, and matters of political decision more generally, within the field of personal—that is, individual—moral challenge. On this point Dworkin has himself

---

51. Compare Thomas Nagel, "Moral Conflict and Political Legitimacy," *Philosophy & Public Affairs* 16 (1987): 215, 233.

[D]isagreements about the morality of nuclear deterrence or the death penalty [compare, of restricting abortion by state power] ... are poor candidates for liberal toleration because they are not matters of individual conduct, which the state may or may not decide to regulate. So no conclusion about what the state should do can be derived from the refusal to justify the use of state power by reference to any particular position on the moral issue. The application of the death penalty or the possession by the military of nuclear weapons cannot be left to the private conscience of each individual to decide.

insisted. In writings apart from *Life's Dominion*, Dworkin has called for constitutional arrangements providing citizens with as much room as possible for "extending their moral life and experience into politics."[52] He has explained broad constitutional rights of political franchise and expression on the ground, in part, that it's of great value for people to integrate political-moral responsibility with the rest of their moral lives, which they cannot do without freedom both to speak their judgments and to have themselves counted in support of them. And further required for each political-moral agent, Dworkin has said, is what he has called "part" or "leverage."[53] As he has explained, "we do not engage in politics as moral agents unless we sense that what we do can make a difference," and it is therefore a goal for constitutional arrangements to "permit anyone who wishes it enough leverage or engagement to make it possible for him or her to treat politics as an extension of his moral life."[54] "Self-respect," he has said, "requires that people participate . . . in the moral argument over the rules under which they live."[55]

Dworkin has sometimes seem poised to justify judicial supremacy on matters of constitutional meaning on the ground that this arrangement actually does better at providing such engagement for citizens, at the level of the political-moral fundamentals, than would leaving constitutional interpretation in the hands of an elected representative body. Judicial review, he has written, "provides a forum of politics in which citizens may participate, argumentatively if they wish, and therefore in a manner more directly connected to their moral lives than voting almost ever is."[56] Expanding on this proposition, Dworkin has more recently urged (in a way that fits nicely with our consideration earlier of the benefits of judicial leadership) that the decisions of the Supreme Court effectively channel and educate public debate on political-moral questions of constitutional dimension, providing it with needed framework, focus, point, and energy.[57] But these observations, however well

---

52. Ronald Dworkin, "What is Equality? Part 4: Political Equality," *University of San Francisco Law Review* 22 (1987): 1, 21.

53. See Ronald Dworkin, "Equality, Democracy, and Constitution: We The People in Court," *Alberta Law Review* 28 (1990): 324, 337.

54. Dworkin, "Political Equality," 21, 22.

55. Dworkin, "Mr. Liberty," 21.

56. Dworkin, "Political Equality," 29; see Dworkin, "Mr. Liberty," 22 ("Individual citizens can . . . experience the moral responsibilities of citizenship better when final decisions involving constitutional values are . . . assigned to the courts. . . .")

57. See Dworkin, "Mr. Liberty," 22.

taken in themselves, cannot provide an affirmative justification for designedly vesting the judiciary with the probable last word on questions
of constitutional meaning. For suppose we had in place a constitutional
reform of the kind I have vaguely described, allowing a popularly
elected body a subsequent and, when exercised, superior word on these
matters. It is hard to imagine how such a system might provide less access or engagement for citizens who seek it than does the adjudicative
practice of the Supreme Court all by itself and easy to see how it could
very possibly provide a good deal more.

   If elected representatives could exercise oversight authority regarding questions of concrete constitutional-legal meaning, citizen-elec-
tors would be directly called to judge the constitutional-legal interpretative judgments of incumbent and aspiring representatives, as those
judgments are manifested in past actions and publicly argued ap-
praisals of past, pending, and potential constitutional-interpretative
events. Judging a representative's constitutional-legal judgment will engage me in the exercise of my own. Even if I ought not judge her judgment "bad" just because I judge the merits differently, still I can hardly
judge her judgment at all without judging her cases for myself. Thus I
would be called as an ordinary voter to this work. Not so under existing practice. Measuring by the terms of intrinsic value—critical interest,
integrity, dignity, ethical challenge, responsibility—does that not give
the advantage to the reform?

   Accuracy

Not necessarily. Participatory process is important to the preservation
of life's intrinsic value as Dworkin conceives it, but so are the legal results that issue from the process. Staying with our main example,
Dworkin and I both think that constitutional protection for procreative
autonomy, specifically in the context of abortion, preserves intrinsic
value. We might also think that independent judges are empirically like-
lier than a popularly representative body to give strong protection to
such rights. If we did have reason to think that giving the people's representatives the last interpretative word would *generally* tend to get us
worse results—results, let us say, less preservative of life's intrinsic
value (or of democracy, or of [whatever you think belongs here])—than
would interpretative government by an independent judiciary, then the
general case would be this: Giving the last word to the people's repre-

sentatives might avoid some frustration of intrinsic value (or democracy, or . . .) at the point of constitutional-legal interpretative process, but it would also increase frustration of intrinsic value at the point of operative constitutional law. If that is the sum of what we think we know now, then intrinsic value provides no sure guide to choice between independent judges and popular representatives as last-word constitutional interpreters—unless, that is, we have general grounds, drawn from experience or from social-scientific theoretical reason, for a compelling prediction that the accuracy advantage either must or must not, in all likelihood, fall heavily in favor of an independent judiciary.

It could be that many people's support of government by judiciary rests at bottom on an apprehension of general reasons for predicting that an independent judiciary having the final word will reach results that are, by a substantial margin, more preservative of intrinsic value (or democracy, or . . .) than will the people's tribunes. Dworkin has said that judicial supremacy is justified "if [it] holds *ex ante* promise of improving the accuracy" of constitutional-interpretative decisions[58] and furthermore has argued that a motivational precondition of accuracy— that political-moral issues be apprehended as ones "of principle" and not "of power alone"—is one that cannot be satisfied, "in any case not fully, within the legislature itself."[59]

Dworkin has a particular reason for the latter assertion, rooted in a certain substantive theory of the political-moral fundamentals, according to which constitutional-legal rights are all, at bottom, rights "that legislation not be enacted for certain reasons."[60] The forbidden reasons are the ones Dworkin calls "external preferences," that is, preferences regarding the fortunes or conditions of persons other than the person who has (and votes) the preference in question. Thus, for example, the reason why laws that disadvantageously classify racial minorities are (according to this argument) rightly held unconstitutional is that we

---

58. Dworkin, "Political Equality," 29. Dworkin has recently said that the theory of government under law as principle "is a theory about what questions must be asked and answered" in applying the Constitution. It is not about "whose answer must be taken as authoritative." Answering the "institutional" question, he continues, requires a "result-driven" standard, and the best institutional arrangement is "the one best calculated to produce the best answers" to basic constitutional issues and secure stable compliance with those answers. Dworkin, "Moral Reading," 25.

59. Dworkin, *Matter of Principle,* 70. Note that my thought-experimental reform would not send constitutional-interpretative questions to "the legislature itself."

60. Ibid., 66.

cannot, in historical American circumstances, "be satisfied that any political body enacting such legislation is relying on a . . . justification" that is free of negative external preferences.[61] Dworkin similarly explains substantive due process or equal protection rights against "morals" legislation, such as laws governing sex in private between consenting adults.[62]

This theory's upshot[63] is that, in many (if not most or all) cases of complaint of violation by lawmaking of constitutional-legal rights, some popularly accountable body stands charged with action in some part prompted—directly or indirectly, wittingly or unwittingly—by illicit reasons. Here we find an apparent basis for Dworkin's insistence that the apprehension of constitutional-rights claims as raising issues of principle, cleanly shut off from facts of power, cannot possibly be "fully" guaranteed within the legislature itself. The idea seems to be that when the constitutional-legal fault lies essentially in motive (perhaps indirect and unwitting), the agent whose motive is in question cannot by any conceivable effort make itself into a suitable judge of the cause.

As applied to our "council of revision" thought experiment, and assuming that the council's members would be responsive to their electoral constituencies, this objection would be tantamount to denying that people can (except, perhaps, very exceptionally) be brought by argument to see the error of what certain representatives of theirs have done in their name—including in that error, perhaps, a failure to recognize unacceptable risk that what they did was inspired by illicit motives. But it seems that would go quite far in the direction of repudiating the very faith in the power of reason and of argument that the constitution-of-principle ideal itself imports and requires. It may not finally be an impossible position for Dworkin, but it ought at least to be an uncomfortable one.

Of course one can always strongly doubt, as an empirical matter, that the mass of the people outside the judicial office can be relied upon to muster, under any institutional arrangements we can devise, the ca-

---

61. Ibid.

62. Dworkin, *Foundations of Liberal Equality.*

63. We need not here trace the theory to its roots in Dworkin's ideas about resource equality as the basis of liberal justice. See generally Dworkin, *Foundations of Liberal Equality.* For an examination of difficulties in Dworkin's derivation of liberal autonomy rights from a theory of justice and equality of resources, see Emily Sherwin, "How Liberal is Liberal Equality?: A Comment on Ronald Dworkin's Tanner Lecture," Legal Theory 1 (1995): 227, 246–50.

pacity and will to take up the interpretative challenge competently and seriously. The question, though, is how one might square such a doubt with a general proposition that life's intrinsic value has its source, for us, in self-creative capacity giving rise to moral rights of responsibility, dignity, and autonomy. The Ronald Dworkin who defends abortion rights, where life or potential life always hangs in the balance, on the ground of the intrinsic value of individual responsibility for moral discernment and choice cannot easily claim belief in deep-seated lack of will or ability, in the mass of the people, for political-moral judgmental engagement. One might still believe that the people at large are unfit for the work of constitutional interpretation, not necessarily but contingently, as presently circumstanced. But present circumstances saliently include the people's subjection to government by judiciary. Unknown is how well they would rise to the challenge, were it to be presented, of interpretative self-government.

Of course this does not make either incomprehensible or indefensible a stance of opposition to the evidently risky experiment. It does make the stance instrumental and calculative—a mixed matter, we might say, of policy and principle. And it does further suggest that the debate over government by judiciary contains a fearful symmetry. Some Americans who question the practice do so, after all, seeking to exchange the safety of guardianship for the dangers of an emancipated life. Thus it is not only one party to this debate—it is not only Dworkin's adversaries (or some of them)—who can be said to prefer a perceived course of prudence to the risks of an arguably nobler venture.

Contributors

Joshua Cohen is Professor of Linguistics, Philosophy, and Political Science at Massachusetts Institute of Technology.

Nancy F. Cott is Stanley Woodward Professor of History and American Studies at Yale University.

Robert W. Gordon is Professor of Law at Yale Law School.

Thomas R. Kearns is William H. Hastie Professor of Philosophy and Professor of Law, Jurisprudence, and Social Thought at Amherst College.

Frank Michelman is Robert Walmsley University Professor at Harvard Law School.

Austin Sarat is William Nelson Cromwell Professor of Jursiprudence and Political Science and Professor of Law, Jurisprudence, and Social Thought at Amherst College.

Michael Taussig is Professor of Anthropology at Columbia University.

Index

Policing (*continued*)
  cal warfare, 19–21, 25, 29; and the
  phobic object, 29–31; and prehistory, 31–34; and taboo, 13, 29–31
Pol Pot, 74
Populism, 50
Pornography, 16, 99–137; and alternative strategies, 132–36; and equality
  and expressive liberty, 99–102; Indianapolis ordinance on, 110,
  112–13, 120, 122–23, 131–32,
  134–35; regulation of, case against,
  115–32; regulation of, case for,
  102–15
Poulantzas, Nicos, 32–33
Prehistory, 31–34
Progressivism, 16, 43, 44, 49–50, 61
Property: and immigration law,
  82n.11, 87; return of, 37–38, 69
Protestants, 92
Public/private realms, 78–79

Quota Act of 1921, 91, 95
Quotas, 52, 55, 91, 95

Race: and affirmative action, 51–53,
  55–56, 61, 63–66; and color blind-
  ness, 51–52, 54, 57, 59, 63, 65, 68;
  and marriage and citizenship, 78,
  83–85, 86–87, 92–94, 96
Racism, 14, 53–54, 56, 59, 61–62; "in-
  stitutional," 67; permanence of, 65;
  and sexism, 103, 107
Radicalism, 62
Raker, John, 94
Rape, 103, 104n.17
R.A.V. v. St. Paul, 135
Rawls, John, 5, 6, 142n.8, 150
Reagan, Ronald, 51, 52, 70
Reage, Pauline, 117–18
Reconstruction, 14, 35–36, 45, 50–51,
  71–72
Repression, 32–33
Resnik, Judith, 7
Responsibility, 17, 156–57, 159, 164
Reynolds, William Bradford, 59n.41

Rodino, Peter, 55–56
Rossi, John, 24–25
Rule of law, 9
Russia, 92
Rustin, Bayard, 62

Sade, Marquis de, 125
Sarat, Austin, 1–17
Scalia, Antonin, 51
Schlusstrich, 40
Schuman Plan, 49
SCLC (Southern Christian Leader-
  ship Conference), 52
Scottish Enlightenment, 41, 49
Sea Islands experiment, 45
Second Reconstruction, 14, 35–36, 50,
  72
Segregation, 54, 60, 68
Self-creativity, 154–57, 164
Sexism, 103, 104, 116, 119
Sexual abuse, 133, 136
Sexual harassment, 103, 133
Sexuality: definition of, and pornog-
  raphy, 105–6; and marriage, 78; and
  "morals" legislation, 163. *See also*
  Eroticism; Pornography
Shackled, 108–9, 127, 128
Shanks v. Dupont, 81, 83, 89
Shklar, Judith, 2, 10n. 48, 10–11
Sing, Ng Fung, 77–78, 92–93
Skocpol, Theda, 66
Slavery, 37–38, 46, 51, 59n.41, 67–69,
  72
Social engineering, 41, 44–45, 75
Social mobility, 43
Sonderweg, 44, 49–50
South Africa, 4
South Carolina, 84
Sowell, Thomas, 57–58, 64
Speech act theory, 111n.43
Stalin, Josef, 74
Statecraft, and prehistory, 31–34
State Department, 44
Statutes of limitation, 40
Stereotypes, racial, 61
Stevens, Thaddeus, 41

Story, Joseph, 80–81, 83
Story of O (Reage), 117–18
Structural approaches, 14–15, 38–39, 42–43, 48–49, 58n.40, 62, 65–66, 70–71, 74–75
Suffrage rights, 82, 88–89
Sullivan, Kathleen, 55, 61, 66
Sumner, Charles, 84

Taboo, 13, 29–31
Taussig, Michael, 13, 14, 17
Taxation, 41, 60, 64
Texas, 33
Texas Chainsaw Massacre (film), 116
Theory of Justice, A (Rawls), 5
Third Reich, 37, 39, 50, 70–71. *See also* Germany; Nazism
Thirteeth Amendment, 84
Thomas, Clarence, 51
Tokenism, 63
Tracking, class-based, 46
Trade unions, 43, 44, 46, 61–62
Transgression, 30–31
Treason, 26
Truth, 5
Truth Commission, 38
Two Live Crew, 118

Unger, Roberto M., 9n.41
Unions, 43, 44, 46, 61–62

Utah, 86, 118
Utopianism, 36, 72n.63

Veterans, 64
Victim, status of, 67
Vietnam, 19, 25
Virginia, 84

Waco incident, 33
Wagner Act, 60
Warfare, mythological, 19–21, 25, 29
War on Poverty, 62
Warrington, Ronnie, 3–4, 7
Weimar Republic, 44, 71. *See also* Germany
West Indians, 57
Whigs, 74
"White flight," 64
White supremacy, 54, 65. *See also* Racism
Whitney, Anna, 133
Wiedergutmachung, 40
Wilson, William Julius, 66
Working class, 44, 66
World War I, 89
World War II, 14, 35–37, 69, 71
Wyoming, 87

Yeoman farmers, 42, 45
Young, Iris, 6n.29, 12

Printed and bound by CPI Group (UK) Ltd, Croydon, CR0 4YY

09/06/2025

14686111-0002